Eat More Ice Cream!
A Succinct Leadership Lesson
for Every Week of the Year

Michael Bret Hood

Copyright © 2015 Michael Bret Hood

ISBN: 1519401701
ISBN-13: 9781519401700

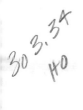
DEDICATION

This book is dedicated to the men and women who choose to serve others.
Although you are not always appreciated and are frequently taken for
granted, your perseverance, your steadfastness and your service despite
challenging and sometimes life-threatening conditions are something that
we all admire, whether we choose to acknowledge it or not.

CONTENTS

ACKNOWLEDGMENTS

This book could not have been completed without the assistance of a number of people. I would like to specifically acknowledge Nancy, Alexandra, Chloe, Cynthia, Tonya, Harold, Carole, Russ, Tim, Mike, Dan, Jerry, George, and many others who gave me the confidence, the ability, the desire, and the help to bring all of these disparate thoughts together.

I Should Have Eaten More Ice Cream!

We had a conversation among colleagues today where we started to discuss work/life balance. The cordial discussion led to the ever-present conflict between earning a living to support a family versus the need to spend time with family. As the discussion went on, a wise colleague stated how his two daughters were now reaping the benefits of his hard work by being able to attend better colleges. Sure he had missed important events in their lives to achieve and promote but without these sacrifices, he would not be in the financial position he currently holds. He was proud that he could provide a great education for his daughters.

When asked if the missed family events were worth being able to provide a better life for his family, he quickly replied that he wished he could have been there for all of his daughters' noteworthy occasions. But to succeed and be a providing father, costs in the form of not being present were dutifully incurred. A single ensuing question altered his perception and perspective immediately. "If your daughters were given a choice of going to a great college or being able to spend more time with their Dad, what choice would they make?" He bowed his head down before looking up again. "They would probably choose to spend more time with Dad." If you make similar sacrifices and perceive that the overriding goal is more important, you very well may be correct. Still, what would your children say if they were given the same choice of being in a better financial position or having a mother and father present at something that was important to them?

My wife and I like to have this conversation every so often where we ask each other as well as our friends this simple question, "If you were on your deathbed, what would you have wished you would have done more of?" Most people have answered the question by stating they would have spent more time with family, but there are exceptions to that rule. For example, my wife, who is very fit and health-conscious, always answers, "I wish I would have eaten more ice cream!" To date, and we have asked this same question to hundreds of people, no one has answered, "I wish I would have worked more."

Every day, we make choices on how to spend our time. While work is a necessity, our priorities sometimes become unbalanced. Jim Collins, the author of *Good to Great* and *Built to Last*, wrote, "For no matter what we achieve, if we don't spend the vast majority of our time with people we love and respect, we cannot possibly have a great life."[1] If everyone did a truly honest self-assessment of our actions compared to our priorities, we might just decide we would be better off eating more ice cream.

---

[1] Collins, J. (2001). *Good to great: Why some companies make the leap--and others don't.* New York, NY: HarperBusiness.

Is Leadership A Choice?

Can you choose to be a leader? Your immediate response is probably in the affirmative. But ask yourself the question a second time only this time, pause and reflect while you give it more thought. Can you truly choose to be a leader?

This question has led to a number of quality discussions involving the role of the leader and the role of followers. While you can certainly choose to take a leadership role in any situation, can you compel people of free will to accept you as the leader of the group? To say yes would mean that the followers of any leader would have no say as to who their chosen representative would be. If you ever saw the movie *Old School* with Will Ferrell, there was a scene where Ferrell's character exhorts a group of partygoers to join him in streaking down a public street. When the camera next pans to a running and nude Ferrell, the audience saw that no one had joined him in the endeavor.[2] Leaders with no followers, like Ferrell, are simply running alone.

---

[2] Phillips, T. (Director). (2003). *Old School* [Motion picture]. United States: Dreamworks Pictures.

Many of us have a desire to lead as well as the skills to do so, but leadership is not as simple as raising your hand. While some leaders emerge because of expertise or because of the situation, most leadership requires effort, investment and sacrifice. The things you do today will determine whether people see you as a leader in the future. For example, do you recognize the efforts of others around you? Are you establishing reciprocal relationships that are mutually beneficial? Are you helping others achieve and meet personal goals? Are you creating a culture of "us," sacrificing some of your personal desires for the betterment of the group? Is yours the voice that says "we can" when others think they can't?

Answering questions such as these will help you understand if you are laying the foundation for becoming a leader in the future. When crisis arrives, people will not necessarily flock to the person who volunteers to be the leader. They won't necessarily gravitate to whoever holds positional authority. Rather, they will act like metal to a magnet. They will seek out the person who lifted their spirits, who allowed them to succeed in their own way, and who appreciatively recognized their efforts even when no one else did. The person who exemplifies these traits will be their leader.

Sometimes leadership starts in a quiet hallway with a friendly conversation. Or maybe leadership starts with a conscious recognition of a thankless job. No matter how or where it starts, people are always looking to find their leader. If you take the time to make an investment in people, you might find that you don't have to volunteer to be a leader. Instead, you will be chosen.

The Carver & the Planter

Have you ever walked on a winding trail through a forest? The respite these trails provide gives leaders a chance to reflect, recharge, and reassess priorities. Recently during one of these walks through the woods, a common sight appeared—one that all of us have seen at some point. On the trunk of a majestic pine tree, someone had carved out a heart with two names in the middle. In that moment, a leadership question formed. As leaders, should we be more interested in making a mark or creating sustainable leadership?

Some people would argue that making a mark is a form of sustainable leadership. A portion of that statement probably holds true. However, upon further inspection of the tree, you see a significant cost associated with the act of leaving one's mark: the etching ripped off a large chunk of the tree bark. A deliberate act put the tree's survival in jeopardy. Does a leader's need to leave a name or mark outweigh the long-term consequences of such an action?

What if we compared the carving of the tree with another

ritual? For instance, some newly married couples symbolically plant a tree to have it grow along with their union. If we contrasted both actions from a leader's point of view, what would we find?

The FBI Academy has a tree that students see as they go outside to exercise. In 1991 four signs hung from the tree and served as sentinels. The words "hurt," "agony," "pain," and "love it," reminded all of us that if we were to be leaders, we needed to make personal sacrifices. Today, that same tree has six additional signs nailed into its trunk.

While the people who hammered the newer signs into the tree had good intentions, closer inspection reveals signatures or class markings inscribed on the backs of some signs. Taking pride in an accomplishment certainly should not bring shame to a leader, but the next time you take a walk in the woods or take a moment to self-assess, ask yourself how you measure your leadership. Is it important for your organization and your followers to specifically remember your name, or is it better to remain unnoticed but never forgotten through the caring lessons you taught the future leaders of your organization?

Therein lies the difference between the carver and the planter. Sometimes the best leaders quietly go about their day planting seeds and watching their trees grow over time. As these new trees grow, they drop seeds, and new generations of trees sprout anew in a continually renewable cycle. In this manner leaders who carve their mark into trees disappear into oblivion when the trees die or heal, while leaders who sow the fields enjoy eternal life.

Lincoln's 1ˢᵗ Rule of Leadership

As soon as you start reading the email, your blood starts to boil. You are being accused, criticized and/or demeaned. Your face turns red. Your body tenses. You can't wait to reply. Fingers sledgehammer the keyboard. Setting the record straight becomes your singular focus. Each word scrolling on screen brings vindication. Finally, you hit the send button and waves of satisfaction wash over you.

In the scenario above, you have just succumbed to an emotional hijacking or amygdala hijacking as coined by Daniel Goleman when referring to the part of the brain that processes feelings.[3] No one likes to be criticized. In fact, our bodies respond to criticism and mistruths by sending more cortisol to our brain. This chemical shuts down the reasoning center of our brains and activates the protection center causing us to perceive greater negativity than actually exists. This stirs the fight or flight reaction that is part of our instinctive behavior.[4]

---

[3] Goleman, D. (1995). *Emotional intelligence.* New York: Bantam Books.

[4] Glaser, J. (n.d.). *Conversational intelligence: How great leaders build trust and get extraordinary results.*

Emotional hijacking is the opposite of emotional intelligence, which is built upon recognizing, understanding, and managing yours as well as your followers' emotions while also utilizing this capability to motivate. If you cannot regulate your own emotions, how are you going to understand and empathize with your followers? If criticism enrages you, how will you ever be able to lead your followers effectively? Shouldn't leaders' motivation originate with the idea of continually growing as a leader instead of disproving the doubts of others?

President Lincoln understood these things. When he perceived criticism, Lincoln followed a self-imposed rule. Just like you, he allowed himself to be emotionally hijacked. Lincoln quickly authored an angry rebuttal, but instead of depositing the letter in the mail, he placed the letter in his jacket pocket. Approximately 24 hours after doing so, President Lincoln retrieved the letter and reread it. Many times, the letter ended up in the garbage with Lincoln understanding how his emotions had compromised his ability to reasonably assess what was being said about him. As much as he hated to admit it, people made valid points and when addressed, these criticisms helped Lincoln to improve as a leader.

The next time you receive criticism, fight the urge to strike back. Resist the effects of cortisol overload. Look deep within yourself and ask if the critique represents an opportunity to improve. Have you ever hit the send button and wished you hadn't?

Climbing the Leadership Ladder: A Leader's Duty to Help Others

If you look back on your career, what were the things that helped you grow as a leader? Did someone take the time to mentor you? Were you given the opportunity to attend different training events? Were you lucky enough to have someone who utilized your strengths but also found ways to improve your weaknesses? Has a leader ever delegated a challenging assignment to you? Did you ever stop and consider the fact that these leaders who assisted on your leadership journey may have sacrificed opportunities for themselves to make you better?

We often have a discussion in class where we debate pursuing opportunities to better ourselves as leaders as opposed to allowing our followers opportunities to grow. Being able to do both at once is probably the ideal answer, but we sometimes fall into traps, some of them self-devised. How many times have you or one of your followers asked to attend a class or seminar? While everyone encourages the opportunity for growth, the statement rings hollow when you or your boss find an excuse to deny the trip. Common refrains such as "You're too valuable to be gone," or "We're just too busy right now" represent lost opportunities and potentially lost leadership credibility. As soon as you or your followers are denied such an opportunity for growth, chances are you soon see someone higher than you in your organization heading off to some exotic place for his/her own training and growth.

How do we get to the point where we find excuses for why our followers cannot improve themselves, but when it comes to us, we have no issues doing whatever it takes to achieve growth? Is this in conflict with our duties as a leader? Do we subconsciously allow our desire to advance and grow to take precedence over the needs of our followers?

Wanting to improve yourself as a leader is nothing to be ashamed of, but we must realize our followers are also relying upon us to assist them on their leadership journey. Sometimes it may be necessary for the leader to put personal desires to the side so that others may grow. Robert Greenleaf, author of *Servant Leadership: A Journey into the Nature of Legitimate Power and Greatness*, asserts, "Good leaders must first become good servants."[5]

A lieutenant in a mid-sized police department captured the essence of Greenleaf's words in his approach to leadership. To him, leadership took the form of a ladder, but not necessarily in the way you would first imagine it. To him, the ladder represented his view of leadership, but the ladder wasn't propped up against a wall or extended ready for him to climb. Rather, this ladder was firmly attached to his back. This leader felt a duty to help his followers. As such, they were frequently encouraged to use the ladder on his back to attain their own goals and follow their own dreams. The leader fully understood there would be those who used his ladder to rise to greater heights and there would be those who would slip and fall, but he would make sure to catch them. If his followers did indeed rise to positions above him in the organizational hierarchy, this was occasion to rejoice, not lament, for the leadership ladder had served its purpose.

Leaders have many obligations but there may be none as important as serving our followers. Service to our followers can mean many things, including providing opportunities for improvement all the

---

[5] Greenleaf, R. (1977). *Servant leadership: A journey into the nature of legitimate power and greatness*. New York: Paulist Press.

way to discipline when needed. Even with that type of service mindset,

aren't we still overlooking something? Going back to the example of

our lieutenant, isn't it possible that as his followers climbed his ladder,

he too was learning from them? Wouldn't that assist him, as well as

you, to grow into an even better leader?

Leadership Is All About the Little Things

We have all suffered through unforgettably bad bosses, but there is usually at least one incredible leader who evokes some of our best memories. Maybe he/she was a mentor, friend, or confidante, but something about them motivated you. You wanted to work harder for them. You wanted to be better for them. If you didn't give your best effort for that leader, you felt guilty. But what was it about that leader that inspired you? Can you put your finger on some identifiable trait that made him/her so different?

You may not be able to explain exactly what it was, but there was just something in the person's leadership that drew you to them. In today's terminology, your best leader would probably be referred to as a transformational leader. Bernard Bass helped provide a modern-day definition of transformational leadership by developing four distinct components: idealized influence (actions speak louder than words), intellectual stimulation (thinking outside of the box), inspirational motivation (exciting the masses, sharing the vision) and individualized consideration (compassionate leader).[6] Numerous studies have shown how transformational leadership is by far the most effective form of leadership practiced today.

A transformational leader is someone who does not rely on carrots or sticks to get his/her followers to accomplish the mission. This leader doesn't lead through fear and intimidation, but rather by respect and compassion. Instead of telling you what to do, this leader allows you to connect the dots and figure things out on your own. A transformational leader is able to empathize with you knowing when to offer encouraging words as well as when to give you a firm push. Oftentimes, this type of leader engages in small, subtle yet powerful gestures that show you how much this leader cares about you.

A sheriff in a small town utilized transformational leadership every Christmas. The Christmas day shift was always loaded with younger officers as shifts were handed out based on seniority. No one wanted to work on Christmas day, but obligations of a police department never take a day off. Roll call occurred every morning at 6:00 A.M. On

---

[6]Barbuto, J. E. & Cummins-Brown, L. L. (2007). Full range leadership. University of Nebraska, Lincoln Extension, Division of Agriculture and Natural Resources. Retrieved July 22, 2015, at
http://www.ianrpubs.unl.edu/pages/publicationD.jsp?publicationId=198

Christmas, the officers were surprised to see the sheriff present and dressed in uniform. As roll call was about to start, the sheriff called out two deputy's names and told them to go home. Unbeknownst to them, they had been previously selected by the sheriff because they had young kids at home. The sheriff told the young deputies that he was going to take their shift for the day and they were not to worry; they would still be paid as if they worked. These deputies went home and had the sheer joy of watching their young children eagerly ripping through presents that Santa had left the previous night.

Will those deputies ever forget what the sheriff did for them? Will they run through a brick wall if the sheriff asked? What little things are you doing to increase the bond between leader and follower?

Carrot & Stick Leadership: Why It's not as Effective as You Think

As a leader, have you ever seen your group stuck in a rut? Did you sense members of the group losing motivation? Are your followers de-motivated because of the pressure and stress in an organization? Maybe your followers have gone into a lull. Have they lost their edge? Are they settling for mediocre performance? Are they failing to give you their best effort? In any of the above situations, how would you turn things around if you were their leader? Most of you probably considered using a form of transactional leadership more commonly known as the carrot and stick. Did you know that using these tools is probably the worst thing you can do as a leader?

On the surface, carrots and sticks seem like an effective tool to rehabilitate and motivate followers, but there are repercussions to the use of transactional leadership. While followers will most likely comply with carrot and stick leadership, what goes on psychologically will surprise you. In a classic study referred to as the candle problem, scientists found that incentives stifled creativity and prolonged the time

people needed to complete certain tasks.[7]

The same logic applies to sticks as well. Enron Corporation, which

was one of the United States' most famous examples of corporate

fraud, had a notorious rank and yank peer review committee system

where each employee was evaluated on formal feedback categories.

Although the program was designed to align employees with Enron's

strategic objectives, it quickly became a means to inhibit contradictory

perspectives. The rankings were subjective and leaders adapted the

feedback ratings to threaten, coerce and punish. If an employee was

ranked in the bottom 15 percent, the employee was immediately

transferred to an area for nonperformers and given two weeks to find

another job in the company or be fired.[8] What effect did this style of

leadership have on motivation and/or morale?

Transactional leadership was a more effective tool in the past when

---

[7] Pink, D. The puzzle of motivation, Ted Talk. Retrieved August 7, 2015, at
http://www.ted.com/talks/dan_pink_on_motivation?language=en#t-792569

[8] Free, C., McIntosh, N., & Stein, M. (2007). Management controls: The
organizational fraud triangle of leadership, culture, and control in Enron. *Ivey
Business Journal*, July/August 2007. Retrieved August 7, 2015, from
http://iveybusinessjournal.com/publication/management-controls-the-
organizational-fraud-triangle-of-leadership-culture-and-control-in-enron/

decisions and performance were routine-based. As the world around us has grown more complex, we are requiring our followers to do more than just follow our commands. We are asking them to think for themselves and to make correct decisions. General Stanley McChrystal, in his book *Team of Teams*, claims success against Al-Qaeda came only after empowering troops to make more of their own decisions.

Using the carrot and/or stick are conventional methods of motivation that are no longer effective. Although we are still drawn to these techniques because of familiarity and ease of implementation, a leader needs to adapt to the needs of their followers. Twenty years ago, you could find a pay phone every few city blocks and cell phones were the size of a small suitcase. Today, you would have great difficulty finding a payphone and cellphones are hand-held devices capable of doing as much as most desktop computers. If we can move out of our comfort zone and adapt to massive technological changes, then shouldn't we be able to adapt to what best motivates our followers?

A Tale of Two Retirements

Have you ever been to someone's retirement party? What was your purpose for going? Was it out of respect? Was it because you truly liked the person retiring? Is it possible you were using the retirement party as a way to get some face time with executives you knew would be present? If we look closer, however, are there leadership lessons that can be learned from retirement parties?

See if you can recall the last retirement party you attended. If you did an honest self-assessment, what was the real reason you went? Once you find your reason, see if you can remember some of the conversations at the party. Were they about work or were they about the person who was retiring? Were the stories being told referencing what the retiree accomplished or were they about how the retiree touched others during his/her career?

Let's compare and contrast two retirement party stories to explore this point. In the first instance, a positional leader announced his retirement after over 20 years of service and planned a grand celebration at one of the nicest venues in the area. This person designated what he wanted as a retirement gift and announcements for the party were placed all over the workplace. After two weeks, six people had signed up to attend. Hearing this, the positional leader put out an order to executives making their attendance at his retirement event mandatory. In the end, people went through the motions but less than 20 people attended and the retiree financed his own gift.

In contrast, another employee in a lower-level leadership role announced her retirement after over 20 years of service. She reluctantly agreed to a party being thrown in her honor. Once again, there were announcements posted all over the workplace. Her party was held at a modest venue and she asked that any donations made in her honor be given to charity. When the date arrived for her party, the room was overflowing with people. The attendees not only gave money to her designated charity but also pitched in and bought her a gift to honor her service to the organization.

Leaders make lasting impressions on their followers. In the first case, the leader had to order people to show up to his party. In the second case, people went because they chose to be there. Doesn't this tell us all we need to know about their leadership styles?

In our classes at the National Academy, we try to come up with ways to describe styles of leadership, such as autocratic, transactional and transformational. While leaders should and do use a variety of styles to lead their people, a transformational leader is able to convey how much he/she truly cares about their followers. In a way, retirement parties can clearly paint a picture of who was and who was not a transformational leader based on the number of people who choose to attend. When it's time for you to retire, do you want to be the leader who orders people to attend your retirement party or do you want to be the leader whose room is overflowing with people who just want to say thanks for making a difference in their life?

Leadership Lies in the Eye of the Beholder

Before you read any further, take a second and compose your definition of leadership. Write it down. Do you like it? What are the chances your definition reads exactly as someone else's? Should it?

By now, every one of us has heard a variety of leadership definitions but how is it that we can never settle on a common version? In some definitions, we make the central focus the ability to influence others to do more than they think possible. Some definitions imply team success while others mention improving corporate performance. Notable leadership experts' definitions range from a primary focus on long-term vision, empowerment, and serving others. Are these definitions correct? Are they incorrect?

By now, we can probably agree that while multiple definitions of leadership have common themes, there are always little details that differ based on who is composing the definition. As leaders, how should we account for these differences and do they matter?

Beauty lies in the eyes of the beholder is a common saying,

which has been attributed, rightly or wrongly, to the philosopher Plato. If we substitute the word "beauty" and plug in "leadership," do we not have the same effect? Leadership means different things to different people. Some people will perform better by being empowered while others would prefer the leader to help them achieve more than they thought possible. No matter the need, each follower has unique expectations for their leader. Therein lies an integral part of any definition of leadership.

Whose responsibility is it to know and respond to follower's needs? An important responsibility of a leader is to know their followers. Can you say that you know what motivates your people? Can you articulate the things that are important in their lives? Would you be able to list the skills and abilities each of them have and then place them in positions to succeed?

Former UCLA basketball coach John Wooden has a quote about leadership, "No one cares until they know how much you care." If a leader can't answer these questions about their followers, how can they ever expect to lead? After all, leadership lies in the eye of the beholder.

The Narrow Path of Leadership & Discipline

Why is it that leaders have difficulty with discipline? Do we not want to hurt people's feelings? Does discipline fill us with negative feelings? Could it be possible that we don't like to discipline others because in some way, it may reflect negatively on our own leadership skills? Is it harder for a leader to discipline followers who are/were friends and/or colleagues? Whatever your feelings are about discipline, the act of disciplining or not disciplining your followers may be the linchpin that decides whether or not you are successful as a leader.

How many times have you served in an area where there were team members who did as little as possible? How did you feel about them? Did they frustrate you with their lack of productivity and/or results? Did you feel like you were forced to take on a more burdensome share of the tasks required for the team? Did you find yourself wondering why the leader didn't fix the problem?

Therein lies the major problem with discipline. Even though a leader may be reluctant to resort to disciplinary measures, there are others who see what needs to be done. Don't think for a second that these followers don't realize they are doing more than their share of work. If a leader does nothing, he/she creates a crack in the ice with followers. The longer discipline is held in abatement, the bigger the crack grows. Eventually, the ice will separate and all remnants of credibility for that leader are lost.

Eighteen people were attending an instructor development class where the students would have to give four interactive learning sessions. The facilitators of the course spent the first day outlining the requirements and teaching the students the concepts of adult learning and instructional design. When it came time to give their blocks of instruction, most of the students did well but there were those who needed remedial assistance. By the third teaching activity, it was clear that one participant was not going to meet the requirements of the course. When told they would not pass, the student decided to go home instead of continuing with the hopes they could attend a later version of the course. After the student's departure, the leader told the class what happened. On the next break, 6 of the 18 students came up to the leader and voiced their approval of the dismissal. According to these students, it was obvious the dismissed student had not performed adequately and the dismissal gave credibility to both the course and the leader.

In the above example, followers noticed who could and could not perform. They were waiting to see if the leader acted or if the leader declined to act. In deliberate inaction, the leader sends a message indicating they are unable or unwilling to administer discipline and this has profound effects on that leader's credibility. A leader who follows through when discipline is needed sends an opposite message and earns more credibility. The next time a situation calls for discipline by a leader, where will you stand?

Attitude Reflects Leadership

Have you ever experienced a boss who made you cringe when you knew he/she was lingering near your cubicle or office? Did you know it was going to be a good or bad day based on whether you saw the boss's car in the parking lot? Is this the kind of boss who micromanages everything in the workplace? How did these experiences impact your motivation and what effects did they have on employee morale?

In a scene from the movie *Remember the Titans*, the team is in turmoil because they refuse to collaborate and assist each other. The team captain confronts one of the characters because the player seems to be acting only in his best interest and to the detriment of the team, but the player gets the last word. As the captain admonishes the player for having a bad attitude, the player tells the captain, "Attitude reflects leadership."[9]

If we stop and reflect on that quote for a second, can we say that the ultimate leader of an organization can have a direct and meaningful

---

[9] Yakin, B. (Director). (2000). *Remember the Titans* [Motion picture]. United States: Walt Disney Pictures.

impact, positive or negative, on the entire company culture? What if that leader doesn't have direct contact with all the members of the organization? Would that change the results?

As we explore this idea, let's take into account two current organizational cultures related by different followers. In the first culture, a chief executive officer recently publicly chastised one of her employees for introducing a new employee to people whom she would regularly work with outside of their organization. When the chief executive officer found out about this, she immediately visited the offending employee. This boss required everyone to get her permission before initiating things on her own. Initiative was not permitted in this arena of micromanagement. The employee who attempted the goodwill gesture on behalf of the new employee was publicly reprimanded for taking initiative. The CEO, whether she intended to or not, delivered a clear-cut message regarding the acceptability of making decisions on your own. What do you think the culture is at this organization and would you ever want to work for a tyrant such as this?

In the second work environment, a leader, who sits in a mid-management position, spoke of a poisonous culture that had prevailed in the agency for over 10 years. Turnover was high and promotions were granted based upon whom you knew instead of ability. When the CEO of the agency was forced out and a benevolent leader took his place, the culture changed almost instantly. This leader spoke with his followers and asked them how they would improve the workplace culture. When they provided valid suggestions, he implemented them. When he couldn't act on their suggestions, he explained why. In a short time, a place where no one wanted to work became a place where no one wanted to leave because the leader set the example not only with his actions but also his attitude.

There have been many studies to show how emotions are contagious. If a leader is negative or positive, the likelihood that followers will mimic these behaviors is high. Whether we recognize it or not, followers are constantly looking at us for the verbal and nonverbal cues, which set the tone for the workplace. If you were a follower, would you rather be led by fear and intimidation, or would you rather be led with respect and compassion?

Leadership Lessons from Psychopaths

If you could choose a leader, what traits would you want them to possess? Would you want a leader to be self-confident? Would you want a leader to know exactly what to say when you are feeling down? Do you like having a leader who senses when something is wrong with you and reacts in just the manner you need? Do you like leaders who have a certain charisma about them? These are certainly admirable traits in a leader but only 1 percent of our society has the exact combination we have described. However if we look a little closer at these traits, we might be surprised at who is capable of possessing them.

According to estimates, psychopaths make up approximately 1 percent of the world population. In a study of corporate executives on a management track to executive leadership positions, psychiatrists Paul Babiak and Robert Hare measured a 3 percent rate of psychopaths in the corporate environment, which means that for every 100 people in your organization, 1 to 3 of them, on average, are psychopaths.[10]

Remember, real world psychopaths can be vastly different but equally

as dangerous as the mythological Hollywood psychopaths, such as

Hannibal Lecter, Michael Myers, and Jason.

Psychopaths initiate an assessment process as soon as they meet

people similar to how we make initial impressions of the people we

meet. Whereas we intend to label or identify people, psychopaths look

at the person through the lens of utility. What can this person do for

me? What if we, as leaders, changed our thought process when

meeting people and instead of labeling and identifying, looked at new

people to see what kind of utility is within them? What are the talents

inside that have yet to be uncovered?

Psychopaths are also some of the most astute observers in the

world. When asked how he picked his criminal victims, notorious serial

killer Ted Bundy stated he could see who would make a good victim by

the way that person walked. Psychologist Kevin Dutton questioned the

belief that psychopaths had such ability so he set up an experiment

---

[10] Babiak, P., & Hare, R. (2006). *Snakes in suits: When psychopaths go to work.* New York: Regan Books.

where 5 college students would walk on a stage, one of them with a red handkerchief hidden somewhere on their body. The audience consisted of 15 college students who scored high on the Self-Report Psychopathy Test, and they were asked to divine which student had hidden the red handkerchief. Over 70 percent of the students correctly chose which student was secretly carrying the red handkerchief. The study has been repeated on multiple occasions with similar results.[11]

What if leaders had that same laser-like focus? Imagine how you would feel if your leader knew exactly what you needed at the exact right time? What would it be like if your leader recognized talent in you that you weren't even aware existed? How much would you appreciate a leader who could see deep inside you and find certain strengths and abilities to which you weren't necessarily aware? What if that same leader cultivated those strengths by giving you stretch assignments to develop those skills? Would that leader, in turn, make you a better leader in the future?

Leaders and psychopaths, although they share similar traits,

---

[11] Dutton, K. (2012). *The wisdom of psychopaths: What saints, spies, and serial killers can teach us about success.* New York: Scientific American/Farrar, Straus and Giroux.

diverge when it comes to followers. Psychopaths need followers to

extract whatever they can for personal gain while leaders are more

interested in helping others reach their potential. Just as we have

learned what not to do from the bad bosses in our lives, we can learn

lessons from the psychopath's assessment process and focus on our

people so that we can find the places, tasks, and jobs where they are

most likely to succeed. How many psychopaths have you come across,

and what lessons did you learn?

The Unintended Consequences of Leading by Example

Are you a leader who believes an essential part of leadership is showing your followers you are willing to take on any task you may ask of your followers? Do you like to join your followers in doing the day-to-day grunt work required by your organization? Do you take pride in being the first person to arrive and the last person to leave the office every day? If so, you are clearly setting an example for your followers, but you might be surprised to find the example being set may not be what you intended.

Clearly, leaders should set a good example for their followers. This is how many organizations indoctrinate their employees into the company culture and how some employees learn. What happens, though, when a leader's intentions don't match with a follower's perception?

For example, have you ever stepped in and just started assisting a follower with one of their duties? Have you ever decided to join your team and take a role as they completed a task without being asked? If you took the perspective of the follower and the leader took these actions, what would you think? Is it possible that the follower could interpret the actions as a lack of faith in a follower's skills and abilities? Could the follower surmise the leader lacks trust in them because the leader is inserting themselves into the task?

A leader in a mid-sized police agency took great pride in being the first one in and the last one to leave on his squad. Working 14-hour days including the weekends became a badge of honor to this leader. This leader actively started to mentor an employee who had leadership potential by participating in many conversations about leadership. When the leader finally asked why the follower had not pursued promotion, the answer surprised the leader. To this follower, the example set by the leaders in the organization required people to live at the office, give up family time, miss important events in their children's lives, and even suffer through divorces all in the name of the job. This follower was unwilling to promote because he wanted to serve not only his organization, but also his family and loved ones. Becoming a ranking leader in the organization, based on the example set, did not match this follower's life priorities, so he consciously chose to forego promotion.

Followers will look to the leader to set the tone, but leading by example may not always be perceived as we intend. We arrive early, stay late, jump in as needed, and try to be teachers and mentors, but maybe we should look more carefully at the decisions we make as well as the unintended results of our actions. While we almost always intend to assist our followers and be the best leader we can be, sometimes those we are trying to lead misinterpret the example we set.

Is Email Response Time a New Way to Measure Leadership?

Have you ever experienced a leader who allowed their ego to take control over their life? Did they become accustomed to people doing everything for them? Whenever these leaders wanted something, did they get it themselves or did they tell someone to get it for them? Did the leader you recall realize that they had created a work environment that was all about them? How do you think that happened?

As we climb the ranks in any organization, we unknowingly become accustomed to a certain sense of power. Where we once did things for ourselves, we now have assistants who take care of these tasks. We quickly justify these perks by acquiescing to those voices telling us we earned this right. Whether we recognize it or not, we start to put distance between ourselves and our followers.

In the book, *The New Psychology of Leadership: Identity, Power and Influence*, the authors claim there are four rules to being a leader for any group of followers. The leader must be the in-group prototype, the in-group champion, the creator of the social identity (why we are together as a group), and the entrepreneur of the social identity (why the world will be a better place if we join together as a group).[12] If a leader has fallen into the trap of allowing his/her ego to grow, substantially, what are the chances that the leader will fit into the four roles listed above?

Professors Ryan Rowe, German Creamer, Shlomo Hershkop, and Salvatore J. Stolfo of Columbia University did an interesting study using emails from the Enron organization to map their social networks. What the professors found was that they could determine who the executives were based solely on email response time and no other data.[13] If you stop and consider their findings, the study starts to make sense. Think about times where you were emailed by one of your superiors. How quick did you respond to the email from the boss? Now think about a time where you emailed your boss. How quick was his/her response in

---

[12] Haslam, S., & Reicher, S. (2011). *The New Psychology of Leadership: Identity, Influence, and Power.* Hove, England: Psychology Press.

[13] Rowe, R., Creamer, G., Hershkop, S., & Stolfo, S. (n.d.). Automated social hierarchy detection through email network analysis. *Proceedings of the 9th WebKDD and 1st SNA-KDD 2007 Workshop on Web Mining and Social Network Analysis - WebKDD/SNA-KDD '07.*

comparison to yours?

When leaders become accustomed to power, it can have negative results in the workplace if unchecked. Leaders can consciously as well as subconsciously buy into the notion that what the leader needs is substantially more important than what the follower needs. If leaders start to prioritize their needs over the needs of their followers, can they satisfy the four rules put forth in *The New Psychology of Leadership: Identity, Influence and Power*? If someone were to check your and your followers' email response times, would they come to a similar conclusion?

Leading Through Generational Differences

Do you find yourself getting frustrated with Generation Y personnel, generally those people born between the years of 1982 and 2004? If I asked you to create a list of the things you liked about Generation Y and the things you hated, which list would be easier to compose and which side would have the most entries? Now take a second and consider an alternative. Do you think Generation Y personnel are frustrated with their Baby Boomer and Generation X leaders? Do you think Generation Y members could come up with their own lengthy list of things they like and dislike about their older leaders? Are we destined to be frustrated with each other forever?

Daniel Goleman spoke of four domains in which true leaders need to excel. The domains, self-awareness, self-regulation, empathy, and interpersonal skills, are all part of a concept called emotional intelligence. Numerous scientific studies, although somewhat disputed, have shown that leaders who score high in emotional intelligence deliver better results for their organizations as well as their followers.[14] If we are going to be leading people across generations, shouldn't we be trying to improve ourselves in these domains?

For example, a leader who is self-aware will understand a new generation will have different life experiences. For example, the 1980 U.S. Olympic hockey team probably brings back vivid memories for Baby Boomers and Generation X, but for Generation Y, the event is something they read about in a history book. Followers from different generations see things from different perspectives. Leaders who are self-aware recognize and utilize these differences to innovate, make better decisions and mitigate some of their own weaknesses.

Inevitably, leaders will be frustrated with generational differences. A good example of this is when a newly promoted Generation Y detective told his captain that his department car was problematic because it had 30,000 miles on it. Ask yourself how you would deal with this young detective who complained that his vehicle wasn't new enough. What are the chances you would have lost your temper? What

---

[14] Goleman, D. (1995). *Emotional intelligence*. New York: Bantam Books.

are the chances you would have kicked him out of your office? What are the chances you would have berated the young detective to teach him a lesson?

The captain did none of this. Instead, the captain agreed there was, in fact, a problem with the vehicle and told the young detective to place the keys on the captain's desk. After the detective complied, the captain went back to his work without saying a word. Eventually the Generation Y detective left the captain's office minus his car keys. A week later, the young detective poked his head back in the captain's office and advised there was no problem with his car after all. The captain pointed to the keys on his desk, which had not moved in a week. The young detective took the keys and became a great asset to the team.

Lessons can be learned in many different ways. In this instance, the leader was able to empathize by understanding a common generational weakness. Even though this captain was extremely frustrated and angered, he self-regulated mitigating his natural tendencies to deliver an important message. The leader also leveraged his interpersonal skills to allow a follower to become self-aware of a flawed request. Can you employ these emotional intelligence

techniques in your leadership style to better serve your followers?

Leaders Can't Afford to Forget Where They Came From

Do you remember the first day on your job? How excited were you? Were you filled with anticipation? Were you full of hopes and dreams, contemplating what you could accomplish in your new position? At what point in your career did you lose that luster or are you lucky enough to still carry that joy today? If by chance your hopes and dreams have ebbed, is there anyone you have blamed for your disappointment?

When asked this question, many people blame executive management for the cultural ills of the organization. Excuses, such as they have no clue what we do every day and they don't understand our perspective, are rallying cries of frustration. If you think back in your career, have you made similar statements about executive management?

Eventually, you conclude things need to change for the better so you start to promote in your organization. You make a promise to do the right thing when you reach the higher levels of your organization. Take a moment to assess where you are today. Are you meeting the goals you set for yourself when you started to promote? If we asked your followers, would they agree with your assessment?

In an unfortunate incident, a criminal assailant killed a young police officer during an arrest attempt. The leader of the police organization, who was due to retire in the next couple of weeks, was promptly notified even though he was on vacation in another state. Funeral arrangements were made and police officers from all over the state came to pay their respects. The only person who chose not to attend the funeral was the officer's police chief, who had decided to remain on vacation. The police chief sent his deputy chief in his stead.

What do you think the follower's reaction was to the leader who chose not to attend the fallen officer's funeral? Do you think the police chief would have made a different decision if he had taken the time to know his people? Is it possible that this chief felt disheartened by the actions of his executives when he was just a patrol officer? What are the chances that this chief started to promote because he wanted to make a difference for line officers who he felt connected to at the time?

Nike made a great commercial with the tag line, "Work before glory." If you listen closely to the message in the commercial, basketball great Michael Jordan says, "It's not about the shoes. It's about knowing where you're going, not forgetting where you came from." Go back in your past and see if you can remember who you were when you started your career. Get out of your ivory towers and go meet the people who are now in the positions you once held. Let them see your face and talk with you.

Years ago, you started your own career. After the exuberance and excitement wore off and the harder edge started to take over, you blamed executive management for all your problems. Do you think it is any different for the people who were hired in the last couple of years? Whom do they blame for their problems and who occupies those executive positions now?

Own Your Actions

When things go wrong, are we normally as hard on ourselves as we are others? Is it possible or even likely that we get more frustrated when one of our followers messes up as opposed to when we make mistakes? As a leader, is that fair? As leaders, aren't we supposed to admit to our flaws and shortcomings?

All of us know we are destined to make mistakes whether we are a leader or a follower. It is part of being human. The difference, however, is that when we make mistakes, we know what we intended to do. When our followers make mistakes, we do not know their intentions or their thought processes unless we ask. Can you recall a time where you did something and convinced yourself that you made a logical error in your decision-making process? How long did the process take to convince yourself the decision wasn't as bad as you initially thought? If you're not careful, you can eventually induce the belief that the mistake wasn't even yours at all. Rather, you acted because someone else erred.

A leader whose company was in deep financial trouble was wooing investors to infuse new cash into the organization. As part of her pitch,

she arranged for the investors to tour one of the company's factories.

When factory workers heard of the impending visit, they stayed after

work with no pay to ensure the factory was in tip-top shape. The very

next day, the leader led the tour but never took the investors inside the

heart of the factory. At her next all employee meeting, the leader

proudly announced that investors had provided the cash needed to

keep the company operating. She expected joy to follow but was

surprised when her workers expressed anger because she had not taken

the investors through the factory. The leader was appalled. After all,

she had just saved their jobs by convincing the investors to provide the

needed cash. Discouraged, she made a few nasty comments to the

employees and left the factory.

Within a week, the leader regretted the way she behaved at the all-

employee meeting. She realized she had only been focused on her

efforts so she started to look at things from the perspective of workers.

Would she have been upset if her leader had ignored their

contributions? Would she have been upset if her leader had not

recognized their efforts to assist the process? Would she have been

upset if the leader had not acknowledged her efforts? After reflecting, she knew she had made a huge mistake. She scheduled a second all-employee conference, got back on stage, and immediately apologized to her workers for the way she acted. She went out of her way to praise employees who stayed late for no pay. She lauded people's efforts in making the factory tour a success. Most important, she stressed how there would be no financing were it not for the contributions given by team members. In closing, she promised to learn from her mistake and to do her best to be a better leader in the future.

Admitting our mistakes is an important facet of leadership. It indicates that we can self-assess, accept responsibility, and overcome our natural inclination to deflect blame. Self-justification of our choices and decisions is a necessary part of life, but what if we continually found excuses for our mistakes? How would our followers perceive us as a leader? Would we be better leaders if we stopped judging ourselves by our intentions and everyone else by their actions?

The Surprising Things Leaders Do

Would you be willing to do something questionable if you were ordered to do so by your leader? Are you comfortable or uncomfortable working in that nefarious area somewhere between absolutely right and absolutely wrong? How far would you be willing to go in support of your leader and your agency? While you may say you or your followers wouldn't be willing to do certain things for their leaders, you may be surprised by how far people will go when subjected to someone who has or appears to be in a position of authority.

Many of us have drawn a line delineating what we will or will not do when asked by leaders or others who are close to us. The line is frequently drawn when a person is asked to do something immoral or illegal. Theorizing what we would do and then being placed in an actual situation may end up in decisions we never thought possible.

For example, a group of police officers was assigned to be drivers for a local political official. Every day, these officers would serve as a protective force for the public official while driving the official around the area so the official could perform the required duties of the political office. In one election cycle, this political official faced a new opponent. As the official and police officers were driving around, the politician saw opponent's political signs in a street median. The politician ordered the police driver to stop the car and to physically remove the opponent's signs, which was a violation of law. The police officers followed direction but were concerned enough to alert their chief. The chief instructed his drivers to do whatever was needed to keep the politician happy. Later, the politician suffered complications from a surgery forcing the politician to carry a colostomy bag. When the bag became full, the politician ordered the police officers to empty the colostomy bag. These officers did as requested and once again, aired their concerns to the chief only to be met with the same response. The only relief for these drivers came when prosecutors found out about the illegal acts and pressed charges.

In this story, were you surprised by the actions of the police officers, especially since they had taken an oath to follow the law? What about the police chief? Would you have made the same decisions for your people if you were the leader in that position? If you were told to pull campaign signs off the street exposing you to felony charges or if you were ordered to change someone's colostomy bag, would you do it?

Most would argue that there would be no possible way we would comply with such requests. However, could it be that we are failing to accurately take into account certain factors that would affect our decision making? How many of you have a monthly mortgage? How many of you have kids who need food, clothing, etc.? How many of you have car payments or other bills? Does your job provide the means to pay these bills? What would happen if you were ordered to do something illegal or well beyond the scope of your job and refusing would mean the loss of your job as well as your income? What if you had no other job waiting in the wings? Would you be willing to give up your house, your car, and potentially the ability to feed and clothe your children or would you stand up to someone who abuses their authority? Leading when things are going well is relatively easy. It is in those times when difficult decisions are required that true leaders emerge and/or sustain themselves.

The Hidden Power of Giving

Remember the last time someone gave you an unexpected gift? Once the initial feeling of gratitude washed over you, did you all of a sudden start to feel a tinge of guilt because you had not gotten a gift for the person who presented the gift to you? Even though you knew it was an act of kindness, you felt you had to reciprocate. Imagine what we could do if we utilized the rule of reciprocity in our leadership style.

There is a field of science called social psychology, which deals with social interactions including their origins and their effects on individuals. What they have found is that some of our gut feelings cannot only be predicted, but they can also be manipulated. If you watch television or browse through items in a grocery store, chances are you have been exposed to a number of social psychology phenomenon trying to get you to purchase certain quantities as well as certain items.

For example, certain religious groups use the rule of reciprocity to garner donations. As one man was walking through an airport, he saw a member of a religious sect. He turned to walk away but the member had already started in his direction. As much as the man tried to get away, the sect member was able to place a paper flower in his hand. At

that moment, the man stopped, pulled out his wallet, and provided a

few dollars to the group member. He threw the paper flower in the

trashcan as he walked away. The religious sect member saw this and

went to the trashcan, got the flower, and looked for the next person to

which he could provide the flower.[15]

Would you have acted in the same manner if you were given the

paper flower? Even though you may say you wouldn't have, there are

many who would have done the exact same thing as the man who

provided the donation. The rule of reciprocity subconsciously compels

us to act in that manner. If applied properly, a leader can also use the

rule of reciprocity. Have you ever led one of those followers who did

nothing but complain?

A leader once told a story about one of those toxic employees who

complained about everything. When the leader tried to make things

better, the toxic employee only found something else to complain

about. The leader eventually realized that the toxic employee would

eventually become a cancer to the team if his negativity were not

---

[15] Cialdini, R. (2007). *Influence: The psychology of persuasion* (Rev. ed.; 1st
Collins business essentials ed.). New York: Collins.

addressed. The leader tried discipline, coaching, praising when the follower did something right and even ignoring the follower but nothing worked. Finally, the leader invoked the rule of reciprocity. When a new responsibility for his section arose, the leader felt his toxic employee would be perfect for the position in that the leader had heard the toxic employee talk about doing similar things on his days off. When the leader notified the follower of his new responsibility, the follower was surprised. Shortly thereafter, the leader noticed a change in this follower's attitude. The follower arrived at work a much happier person. In time, the follower thanked the leader for granting him this assignment and stated that because of this, the follower felt he had a duty to the leader, which resulted in a complete turnaround in attitude. Eventually this toxic employee became a positive member to other followers in the organization.

The rule of reciprocity will not always work with every individual. Some employees will be able to accept an unexpected gift and continue as if nothing happened. Still for many of us, the unexpected gift provides a psychological compulsion to reciprocate. These gifts can be tangible or intangible; as studies have shown, the rule also applies when people share personal stories or assist in times of unexpected personal crises. In any instance, a leader who takes the time to understand the

wants and needs of their followers may be able to inject the rule of

reciprocity to turn around a toxic follower.

How Great I Am

In Greek mythology, Narcissus, a hunter, had the gift of extreme beauty. In the story, a mountain nymph espied and professed her love for him. Narcissus shunned her as he did everyone drawn to his perfect visage. This left the mountain nymph with profound sadness. Nemesis, the Greek god of revenge, saw what happened to the mountain nymph and lured Narcissus to a pool of water. Once there, Nemesis brought him to the water's edge where Narcissus gazed at his reflection for the first time. Failing to realize he was looking at his own image, Narcissus fell in love with himself. Upon realizing that his love never could be satisfied, Narcissus committed suicide.

Like Narcissus we all can succumb to our own perceived greatness as leaders. How many times have you encountered so-called leaders quick to boast about their accomplishments? What about so-called leaders who go out of their way to show you an accolade or prominently display an award? What about pseudo-leaders who always play the role of the victims, never identifying themselves as the potential cause of the problem? These types of people look in the pool of water, like Narcissus, and see pure beauty in the form of their perceived leadership abilities. They fall in love with themselves, and whatever leadership ability they had—if any—crumbles. Could this happen to you?

In our leadership classes, we often have a long discussion about why we tend to judge ourselves by our intentions, yet evaluate everyone else by their actions. The idea of judging oneself critically is not easy. We often discover things we would like to ignore, but as leaders, critical self-evaluation is essential to gaining followership. Do you remember leaders who continually failed to honestly evaluate themselves, and what did you think of them?

In the coming days or weeks, try to count how many times you use the words "I" and "my" and, then ask yourself if you should be using the words "we" and "our" instead. If you are in a meeting with your boss or a colleague and something has gone wrong, see if you find yourself defaulting to the use of "you" and "them" when explaining problems. Challenge yourself by doing deep self-reflection and determine if "they" are truly the problem or if you have intentionally misjudged your actions by looking only at what you intended to do. Uncomfortable as it may seem, these are moments where true leadership can be forged.

As leaders we all should take a moment to look into a mirror and study what we see. We surely will find some beauty in the reflection before us, but, unlike Narcissus, we must look beyond the first things we see. We must get past the beauty and find the blemishes. Accepting our beauty, as well as our flaws, will allow us to avoid the fate of Narcissus and, instead, become the leaders we should be.

Devil's Advocate: A Leader's Best Friend

Have you ever spent a significant amount of time coming up with a strategy for your organization? Did you think about the positives and negatives of going with such a strategy? Did you rework the policy or procedure until you thought you had it just right? Were you pretty sure you had all angles covered when you announced the strategy to your followers? How did you feel when someone immediately questioned the viability of your strategy upon the announcement of implementation?

When leaders make decisions, they often try to take into account all relevant factors, but things such as implicit biases, perceptions, and previous experiences affect the decision-making process whether we want them to or not. What can be worse is that once we make our decision, we often stick to that decision, even in the face of contrary evidence because we have a psychological need to be consistent with what we say.

In a classic study of racetrack bettors by Robert Knox and James

Inkster, once the bettors placed a bet on a horse, they expressed much more confidence in their horse's chance of winning the race than prior to placing the bet.[16] Just like the racetrack bettors, as soon as you make up your mind and commit to a decision, you have a difficult time going in a different direction. This is why frustration is normally your first reaction to someone when they question your plan.

What is the likelihood that you, in fact, considered every potential possibility that could affect your policy or procedure? Is it possible that your new strategy has a few flaws that went unrecognized? Would you rather be right or would you rather implement the proper strategy for your organization?

Kodak used to be a dominant company in the photography field. In fact, Kodak invented the first digital camera but didn't actively pursue it because it would have cannibalized its' core business. When digital media started to emerge, Kodak executives quickly dismissed the technology arguing that film would always be the preferred medium. As digital media grew, Kodak executives continued to insist they were

---

[16] Cialdini, R. (2007). *Influence: The psychology of persuasion* (Rev. ed.; 1st Collins business essentials ed.). New York: Collins.

correct in their prediction. It has taken a long time for Kodak to recover and some will say that they were never able to catch up.[17]

Another company found it was having trouble hiring the right people. Every time they went through the interview process, they felt they had found a good fit for their organization. More often than not, the person did not work out for various reasons. Instead of the continual churning of new hires, they developed a new process to analyze their candidates. If they selected six candidates as finalists, two of the candidates were assigned to each person on their three-person hiring panel. As was the norm, they were supposed to go over the resumes and find the strengths of the applicant. In addition to that duty, however, the three panelists were also assigned two of the other applicants, but in this case, they were supposed to study the resumes and find the weaknesses in the candidates. Instead of only looking for a candidate's strengths, the panel was forced to also consider their weaknesses when making their decision. This resulted in increased retention rates and a much improved work culture.

---

[17] Pachal, P. (Jan. 20, 2012). How Kodak Squandered Every Digital Opportunity It Ever Had. Retrieved April 4, 2016 from the Internet at http://mashable.com/2012/01/20/kodak-digital-missteps/#tSTU2f0m9Zq0

In the first scenario, Kodak failed to install a mechanism where someone played the role of the devil's advocate highlighting the problems with their strategy. The second company, however, realized there were problems in the hiring process and utilized a devil's advocate to consider potential problem areas with a candidate instead of only focusing on strengths. This led to vastly improved results.

There are others who have recognized the importance of devil's advocates as well. President Kennedy installed his brother, Robert, after the failed Bay of Pigs invasion because he realized he had not properly considered all the potential outcomes. Robert Kennedy was told to find out the President's position on a topic and argue the opposite even if Robert agreed with the President on the issue. By making Robert his devil's advocate, President Kennedy was trying to ensure he considered as many perspectives as possible before making a decision.

A devil's advocate may be one of the most disliked people in an organization but the value they provide is exceptional. They are the ones who are looking at things from a different angle. They actively apply different perspectives looking for the problem areas that may have been overlooked by originators. If you, as the leader, declare your own devil's advocate, prepare to be frustrated but also understand that this person will prevent you from making some mistakes you may later regret.

The Bully, the Puppeteer, & the Coach

If you go back in your career and recall the different people who held leadership positions, how many of them would you label true leaders? How many of them would you rate as bad bosses who simply held a supervisory position? Estimate the ratio of good leaders to bad bosses in your career. Are you surprised by this number? Now think of the best leader you ever had. Once you have a face in mind, do the same task but remember the worst boss you ever had. Which face came to mind the quickest?

For most of us, the bad boss examples came to mind much more quickly than the good leader. In all likelihood, multiple faces popped into your head when considering the bad boss. Why is that? Are we, as human beings, geared towards negativity or are bad bosses more memorable because they teach us what not to do as a leader?

Chances are you have encountered bosses who think positional power is equivalent to leadership. Usually, these people are quick to remind you of their positional dominance. This bully thrives on fear and intimidation forever trying to assert their authority over their subordinates. The bully, however, is blind. If fear and intimidation are the bully's main tool, would you take initiative on any project or would you simply do as little as necessary to avoid the bully's wrath?

If bullies weren't bad enough, how do you avoid the puppeteer? This is the manager serving as a pseudo-leader who convinces you that he/she has your best interests at heart only to betray you once you have served your purpose. This boss has no problem accepting credit and dispersing blame. This manager quickly loses all trust and credibility. How did you like working for someone who had selfish interests? Did you volunteer suggestions when you saw things going wrong or did you keep quiet hoping your manager would receive his/her comeuppance?

Somewhere hidden among the bullies and the puppeteers are the good leaders you recalled. These people tend to go unnoticed because they are quick to step aside and let others take the credit. In some instances, you probably didn't understand their importance until they were gone. These leaders are the ones who allow you and others to fail, to try, and to succeed. They catch you when you fall and they help you grow. Was the work environment different with this leader?

In almost every work environment, we can find all types of personalities who attempt to lead us, though it is easy to see which style is most effective. Imagine if a bully, a puppeteer and a coach asked you to perform the same task. Which person would get the better product? Having answered that question, which type of leader are you?

Shared Sacrifices: Leaders Doing More Despite Having Less

Have you ever been given the directive, "We're going to have to do more with less"? Maybe you have been forced as a leader to pass this mantra on to your followers. How did the conversation go when you heard the statement or had to deliver it? Were you met with frowns, sarcasm, and/or anger? Were your followers happy with the proclamation?

Government, as well as private sector, employees have been hearing the do more with less mantra for quite a while now. Organizational leaders have learned repetition of the phrase does not make it more palatable. The overriding perception is that we are asking our followers to work harder for the same or, in some cases, less pay. Is that something you would want to hear?

So how should a leader respond to the complaints? Should the leader take on more responsibility to alleviate the burden of employees? Should you empathize with your followers? Should you acknowledge the issue or should you avoid it? What steps, if any, can you take as a leader to ease the burden of higher expectations?

In his book, *Leaders Eat Last*, Simon Sinek highlighted the efforts of a leader named Bob Chapman who was the CEO of Barry-Wehmiller during the financial crisis of 2008. Chapman and Barry-Wehmiller were faced with a 30 percent reduction in orders almost immediately. Many people in this situation would have resorted to layoffs because there were drastically fewer orders to fill. Chapman resisted common practices. Instead, Chapman devised a plan where everyone in the company would take four mandatory 1-week furloughs during the year. When Chapman announced the plan, he told his employees it was better that everyone suffered a little pain rather than some sacrificing their job. As the policy was implemented, a funny thing happened. As you would expect, there were employees in better financial situations to survive missing paychecks. Because Chapman was a leader who promoted collaboration and followed through in his actions, some employees in a better financial position voluntarily took additional weeks of furlough so that some of their less financially secure colleagues could continue to work and receive a paycheck.[18]

While this collaboration may have still occurred absent a benevolent leader, studies have shown that emotions, attitudes and behaviors are contagious. There is a reason why the oft-repeated phrase, "The leader sets the tone" is so prevalent. In social psychology, there is a concept known as the social proof theory, which argues that people are more willing to do something after they see another person do it. Social proof theory is why you see bartenders with tips jars showing $5, $10, and $20 bills in the glass and why street performers always line their instrument cases with change and paper currency. In the Barry-Wehmiller case, Chapman set the tone by sharing the sacrifice and his followers mimicked the behavior.

Whether you realize it or not, your followers are watching your every move. They are looking for the cues that set the organizational culture. When times of need arise, are you going to be the leader who sacrifices others or are you going to be the leader who shares in other's sacrifices?

---

[18] Sinek, S. (n.d.). *Leaders eat last: Why some teams pull together and others don't.*

To Delegate or Not to Delegate: An Important Question

Do you sometimes feel overwhelmed at work? Are people coming at you from all directions asking for this and that? Do you often wonder how you are ever going to get all the things accomplished that need to be done? Do you sometimes wish there was more time in the day? How often do you find yourself thinking about work when you are at home? If you answered yes to some or all of these questions, maybe it is time for you to rethink your leadership strategies.

When people are asked to list their leadership weaknesses, most responses include lack of delegation. Leaders frequently express how hard it is to go from being the person who does to being the person who oversees. We are used to being top performers, but now our job as leaders consists of coaxing top performances out of others. Why is it so hard for us to adapt?

When a task is delegated, we allow others to take control of something for which we are ultimately responsible. In discussions, people who have listed delegation as a weakness have offered similar versions of these excuses. "If I do it, I know it's done right the first time." "My people are too busy." "It's just easier to do things myself." What do you think about these statements? Are they legitimate reasons to keep work or are they a communicating the message that the leader does think his/her followers have the ability to do the task and/or the leader does not trust his/her followers to do the task correctly? The preceding statement probably doesn't indicate your true feelings about your followers but actions speak louder than words.

Let's reverse roles for a second. Do you think your followers see how busy you are? Do they see you struggling to keep up with tasks? Do they see you staying late at work? Are they getting texts and/or emails from you late at night? If they notice these things, then they are probably asking why the leader doesn't delegate some of his/her work to them. Without an explanation from the leader, followers quickly wander to their own conclusions, which often lead to personal dissatisfaction.

The lack of delegation can also inadvertently deny followers a chance to grow as leaders. A student, prior to taking a lengthy leave of absence, was preparing to be away from his department for 10 weeks. This leader had a laundry list of tactical, operational and administrative tasks that came with leading a narcotics trafficking task force. As he made a list of things he had to delegate, he came across his most hated task, logging administrative subpoenas. Right before he left, he asked his followers which duties they would like to perform while he was gone. To his surprise, one of his followers immediately came up to him and specifically asked to take over the task of logging administrative subpoenas. All this time, the leader had someone who wanted to do his most hated task.

Delegation is certainly not a way for a leader to dump his/her most unwanted and boring tasks. Rather, delegation should be something a leader leverages to challenge his/her followers, help them grow, and create more time for the leader to serve in a coaching/mentoring role. In a Fortune 500 executive survey, 70 percent of respondents indicated a stretch assignment was the single most important factor in growing their leadership. If you keep these stretch assignments, where are the opportunities for your followers to grow?

As leaders, we can hide behind walls and convince ourselves we are doing our followers favors by keeping certain tasks to ourselves. In reality, we are fooling ourselves. Although we don't often acknowledge it, we sometimes refuse to delegate because we are afraid our followers may do the task better. Is that necessarily a bad thing? True leaders take joy in the success of their followers while also understanding that followers have the ability to teach leaders new ways of doing things. In the end, everyone learns. So if certain tasks can challenge your followers and help make them better leaders, why aren't we delegating more of them?

Everyone Agrees With Us (Or So We Think)

As a leader, you understand the importance of obtaining buy-in from your followers so you have empowered them by allowing them to vote on a new policy. Of the two choices, the correct answer is obvious. You have no doubt your employees will vote the correct way. Yet when the results arrive, you are shocked to see your followers have chosen the other option. How could you have miscalculated so badly?

You have likely fallen victim to the false consensus effect, otherwise known as the false consensus bias. The false consensus effect is the tendency to overestimate the extent to which your views are typical of most people. We tend to be egocentric in our decision-making processes. Our reference points, even when assessing the knowledge, skills, and abilities of others, are derived from our experiences and our perspectives. As a result, we tend to look at our choices more favorably than others and prefer our solutions to problems, believing our opinion is the majority view.

Researchers named Daniel Katz and Floyd Allport proved this theory when students were queried as to whether they cheated on a test. Those who admitted to cheating gave a significantly higher estimate of fellow cheaters on the same exam than those who did not admit to cheating.[19] If we do something, we automatically feel like everyone else would do the same.

Have you ever run across someone who is exactly like you? Unless you're a twin, it is unlikely, but as leaders, we project our logic, beliefs and expectations on to others like ranchers brand their cattle. We neglect the fact our followers have had different experiences which have produced differing perspectives. What we see and feel is not the same as what someone else sees and feels.

A leader once told me he hated a job requirement so much that he waited until the last day of every month to complete it. When this leader took a temporary leave of absence, a follower approached him and requested the opportunity to do this very same task indicating he had always loved that part of the leader's job. The leader falsely believed everyone would hate the task when, in reality, a follower had a different perspective.

---

[19] Kahneman D., Slovic, P. & Tversky, A. (1982). *Judgment under uncertainty: Heuristics and biases.* Cambridge: Cambridge University Press.

As tempting as it may be, we cannot stamp our motivations, beliefs, and interests onto our followers. If we allow ourselves to get frustrated because followers don't seem to care as much as we do, work as hard as we do, or approach tasks in a different manner than we do, we fail as their leader. Just because you see things one way doesn't mean the world or your followers have the same opinion.

A Leader's Actions Speak Much Louder Than a Leader's Words

Would you agree that the leader sets the tone for an organization, a group, and/or individuals depending on their position? Aren't leaders supposed to influence their followers in positive ways? Do we, as leaders, always know how and when we influence others? Is it possible we can influence our followers in ways we don't always recognize? Is that a good or bad thing?

Many definitions of leadership include having the ability to influence others. Influence can be accomplished in both positive and negative ways. Many leaders strive to influence their followers through words as well as actions. While we often focus on what we say to our followers to motivate and set the example, the more powerful message is frequently delivered through a leader's nonverbal actions.

In a classroom exercise, students are tasked to judge the guilt or innocence of a fictitious person given a set of facts. The decision must be unanimous. As the students begin their deliberations, it isn't long before someone assumes the reins as the leader and starts to direct the conversation. This student will more often than not immediately announce his or her position on guilt or innocence. One leader even went as far to say, "How many people believe the suspect is guilty and how many people have come to the incorrect conclusion the suspect is guilty." When that leader announces his or her position or makes statements similar to the one quoted, there is a distinct and tangible effect on those who have taken the opposite position of the leader. You can see those whose decision opposes the leader's stated point of view look around the room to see if they have any allies. Oftentimes, these same individuals start to immediately shrink in their chairs. Once their position is publicized, it isn't long before emotions and verbal and nonverbal behaviors start to denigrate their positions. What eventually happens is that most people, instead of calmly trying to persuade each other to reach a unanimous agreement, start to become more attached to their original stated position. Even the leader is not immune to this phenomenon. Despite publicly stating they will be fair to those who dissent, their nonverbal behaviors send a different message. When the students review what had happened, many of them are unaware of the actions they took and the pressure they placed on those who didn't share the majority opinion.

If the leader hadn't announced his or her position from the outset or if the leader had taken a more balanced position, would the dynamic have changed? Is it difficult for someone to go against the opinion of the leader? Should it be hard for followers to offer their ideas even though they may conflict with the leader's stated position? As a leader, do you want your actions to stifle followers' dissenting opinions?

Once a leader announces his or her position on a topic, it has an undeniable effect on followers, whether the leader wants it to or not. Norbert L. Kerr and Robert J. MacCoun performed a research study and found that juries who utilized the public polling method where a defendant's guilt or innocence was openly announced in the jury room were more likely to develop into a hung jury than those juries who utilized a secret ballot to determine the defendant's guilt or innocence.[20] Psychologists have shown many times that once we take a

---

[20] Kerr, N., & Maccoun, R. (1985). The effects of jury size and polling method on the process and product of jury deliberation. *Journal of Personality and Social Psychology, 48*(2), 349-363.

public position, we are very hesitant to go against that position.[21] If we inject emotion into the equation, we are even less likely to change our minds. The next time you lead a meeting or gather your group together, maybe it would be best if you solicited your followers' opinions first before you provide your own.

---

[21] Cialdini, R. (2007). *Influence: The psychology of persuasion* (Rev. ed.; 1st Collins business essentials ed.). New York: Collins.

Finding Your Leadership Ground Wire

Have you ever encountered people who, after they were promoted, let the power of the position go to their head? How quick did they get used to the entitlement? Did their ego grow substantially? When they spoke, did you hear the word "I" over and over when talking about the successes of the group? Have you ever caught yourself engaging in this type of behavior?

As leaders promote to higher positions in an organizational command chain, they can find themselves growing accustomed to others serving their needs. When leaders move higher in command structure, there are frequently others who try to attach themselves to those leaders hoping they can follow that leader into higher organizational positions themselves. Therefore, an inherent interest exists for that person to do his or her best to please the leader. What are the chances that this person ever offers an honest assessment of the leader's abilities and decisions? Over time, leaders can unconsciously start to expect this behavior from all of their followers and resist sound ideas and advice, as it is contrary to what the leader believes.

In addition, success breeds confidence. When leaders perform, their groups normally meet stated goals and objectives. This leads to compliments, praise, recognition, and/or awards from upper layers of management. Even though leaders may be quick to deflect praise to their group members, the awards and recognition start to become embedded in our psyche.

It is doubtful that any good leader wants success to go to his/her head yet if asked, all of you could recall experiences where you saw such an event with a leader in your organization. So what steps can we take to make sure we do not succumb to overconfidence?

There was a leader who knew he had a tendency to be overconfident after successful endeavors, so he found a way to counteract the problem. With every success, he sent an email message to one of his old high school friends. After getting them up to date on his life, he would remind that friend of a time where they did something embarrassing. The intent was not to denigrate an old friend, but rather, it was to evoke a response. Sure enough within a day or two, his inbox had a reply with an equally embarrassing story of something he had done in the past. This process reminded him that he was never as good as he thought he was and this helped him stay grounded as a leader.

Sometimes, however, we are blind to our egos. In these cases, another leader found a way to make sure she could protect against the times her self-assessment failed. She found a trusted confidante, which could be a peer, follower, or superior. She then empowered this confidante to confront her when the confidante felt like she was letting the power of the position get to her head. Every so often, her confidante would pop into her office and tell her that she might want to look in the mirror. This was their code to get her to self-assess and when she did, she often found the confidante to be spot on.

As leaders, we take great steps to ensure we are serving our followers to the best of our abilities. However, we are human beings prone to mistakes and not always seeing our world clearly. Utilizing friends and confidantes can help keep us in check when we succumb to our frailties. Chances are, these friends and confidantes would be more than happy to reel you in or remind you of some long ago story you probably would like to forget.

Sticking Your Neck Out: How Group Dynamics

Can Affect Leaders

Have you ever complained about a leader not having enough of a spine to do the right thing? Is there an instance where one of your former bosses should have stood up for you, but didn't because he/she did not want to make waves in the organization? Are there times in your life where you can recall stifling an objection or criticism because everyone else in the room loved the idea, product, or proposal? If you answered yes to any of the preceding questions, you may have succumbed to the power of the group dynamic.

In a classic scientific study, a reference line and three comparison lines were shown to a group of people. Participants were asked to identify whether Line A, Line B, or Line C was the same length as the reference line. One could easily see that one of the three lines was the match, but the study really wasn't about finding a comparable to the reference line. As confederates in the experiment declared a certain line to be the match, the one person who was not part of the fix watched with great surprise. When the question finally got to the unsuspecting participant, he/she chose the same incorrect line as the group 33 percent of the time even though the line chosen clearly did not match the reference line. When this experiment ran multiple trials with the confederates intentionally giving incorrect answers, the unsuspecting party conformed to the group's incorrect answer at least once 75 percent of the time.[22] Why did this person purposely choose an incorrect answer if he/she instinctively knew that same answer to be wrong?

As human beings, we have a tendency to follow what others do and mimic the behavior. We have an aversion to going against the group. The more the unsuspecting participant heard people select an incorrect line as the match, it made them study the picture over and over again. Each time the participant came to the same conclusion, but with all of the other participants choosing a different line, pressure mounted on the unsuspecting participant to conform to the will of the group.

Some of you are surely saying that this scenario would never

---

[22] Haslam, S. A, Reicher, S. D., Platow, M. J. (2011). *The new psychology of leadership: Identity, influence and power.* New York, NY: Psychology Press.

describe you. You would be the exception to the rule and go against the group no matter what everyone else said before you. Maybe you're right and you would be in the percentage that spoke up, but if we self-assess, we also might be able to find a time where we didn't say something when maybe we should have. It's easy to say you would take a stand in a theoretical situation, but when such a stand is real and involves some form of personal jeopardy, like the risk of losing a job, would you be as quick to act as you think?

As a leader, do you have followers who count on you to do the right thing even when there are risks involved? Do you have the courage to say something unpopular to both your followers as well as your leaders if necessary? Are you willing to stand alone knowing what you are doing is the right thing even when others, including friends and colleagues, are unwilling to back you as you stick your neck out? If you answered these questions affirmatively, then fight the urge to be the one who blends into a crowd and be the leader who does the right thing.

A Leader in Name Only

Why are we so reluctant to blame ourselves when things go wrong? Is it our natural inclination to deflect responsibility? Are we afraid to discover that some things may be our fault? What happens to our followers when they see us resort to excuses when problems arise? Is that the kind of behavior followers expect or want from their leader?

In a recent public forum debating the customer service issues plaguing a governmental agency, the leader attempted to assuage the public concerns by offering an excuse. According to the leader, the local government was too generous to its employees by offering an abundance of sick leave. This, in turn, caused substandard service due to the fact that on any given day, 25 percent of the workforce was out sick. The remedy for the questionable customer service, according to the leader, was to drastically reduce approved employee sick leave forcing them to come to work. How would you react if your leader made a similar statement in a public forum?

Is it possible that employees in this agency were unmotivated government workers who, without the real threat of losing their job, did as little as possible, causing customers to suffer? Is it also possible that the leader's style led followers to perform minimally acceptable work and to avoid the workplace at all costs? If you were the leader, which excuse would you be inclined to pursue?

We would most likely choose the first option because we can identify hypocrisy in everyone but ourselves. These blind spots cause us to unconsciously preserve our egos, allowing us to rationalize conflicting information in a positive manner.[23] Therefore, the reason for failure is not at the feet of the leader but, rather, at the feet of others.

One of the elements of emotional intelligence is self-awareness. If we maintain so many blind spots, then is it possible we can ever effectively self-assess? A company found a blind spot with hiring. Many of their new employees didn't fit the culture and executives wondered why they were making so many mistakes. In an attempt to self-correct, human resources personnel changed the review process. Instead of picking out only the positive traits on candidates' resumes, they asked their reviewers to also find reasons why the candidate wouldn't fit the corporate culture. By looking at the positives and the negatives, the

---

[23] Tavris, C., & Aronson, E. (2007). *Mistakes were made (but not by me): Why we justify foolish beliefs, bad decisions, and hurtful acts.* Orlando, FL: Harcourt.

reviewers were able to avoid falling in love with a candidate who had plenty of foreseeable culture issues. You can adapt this to your decision-making processes by finding a "devil's advocate" or by considering reasons to go against your natural inclinations.

A second leader agreed to a 360-degree evaluation and was surprised by the responses. His followers had alerted him to a number of weaknesses he never knew existed. Knowing that he would likely fall back into old habits, he developed a system wherein a confidante could silently alert him to instances where he fell back into bad habits. They agreed upon a gesture as a way for the confidante to alert the leader when he was falling back into traps. If you have someone you trust, you can easily come up with a system where you can be alerted without anyone knowing.

It's easy for leaders to sit behind their desk and blame others for a group's problems, but leadership is not always easy. As a leader, would you strive to become a better servant or would you expect followers to adapt to your leadership style? Would you ignore a negative work culture with the belief that some people can never be motivated or would you constantly try to engage followers and make the work environment positive? Would you only look for weaknesses in followers or would you first examine your performance as their leader? Leaders who offer lame excuses like denying people the benefits granted to them are operating in an illusory state where self-justification overcomes common sense. Are you willing to take a hard look in that mirror to determine if the reflection reveals a true leader, or would you rather ignore what you see and try to perpetuate an illusion?

Improving Your Leadership by Maintaining Connectivity

Is your organization so big that it is impossible for everybody to know each other? Does your organization have multiple locations staffed by different people? Are members of your organization present in different states and/or different countries? If you are in a smaller organization, do you ever feel like there are only so many people who can relate to the decisions you have to make as a leader? Would you be surprised to know that if you answered yes to any of these questions, these facts could have a substantial effect on your decision making as a leader?

In some instances, it is impossible for leaders to know everyone in their organizations. In multinational corporations, there may be thousands of employees who have never set sight on the leader's face. If that is the case, is it possible for leaders to make personal connections with their followers?

Smaller organizations can have similar problems with

connecting to followers. Studies have shown that as we rise in organizations, our peer groups start to shrink. This is especially true in organizations that have a limited number of supervisory positions. When difficult decisions arise, it may be difficult for leaders to find peers who can mentor and help guide them. In isolation, these leaders can become frustrated and appear distant to followers.

If leaders are disconnected, they start looking at their followers as numbers, assets, and other abstract items. With no personal connection, it becomes easy to dehumanize them and make decisions to their detriment. All of a sudden, pursuit of efficiency or the bottom line becomes the main focus of the leader. But for each cut or policy change a leader makes, there is usually a net human cost.[24]

Recall the case of Enron, the energy exchange conglomerate out of Texas who collapsed when a massive financial fraud was discovered in 2001. In the summers of 2000 and 2001, California suffered through an alleged energy crisis where providers could not provide enough electricity for the consumers, causing rolling blackouts. At least one

---

[24] Sinek, S. (n.d.). *Leaders eat last: Why some teams pull together and others don't.*

person died during this time. Investigators later discovered there was no energy crisis during that time. Enron traders were manipulating the energy market to make more money by intentionally withholding electricity from the grid. In recorded conversations, Enron traders were caught laughing about the tragic events in California.[25] To the Enron traders, their leaders had taught them that consumers were a commodity and not someone's father, mother, or grandparent.

In contrast, consider a particular leader at a very large police organization. This leader knew he would never be able to personally meet and greet every new employee when they initially began working for the department. Still, he wanted to make some kind of connection with them. The leader instructed his administrative personnel to forward the very first payroll statement the new employees would receive. When he got them, he took the time to handwrite a personal note to each employee telling them how he looked forward to meeting them and working with them for a number of years. The gesture was small but certainly not inconsequential.

---

[25] Roberts, J. *Enron Traders Caught on Tape,* CBS News, 6/1/2004 – Retrieved August 30, 2015, at http://www.cbsnews.com/news/enron-traders-caught-on-tape/

As you navigate your day as a leader, do you find yourself sitting in your office or out meeting with investors, clients, and/or other people outside of your organization? When you are present at your headquarters or visiting one of your satellite offices, is most of your time spent meeting with command staff members? What do you think would happen if you took a few moments out of your day to just walk around and greet the hardworking followers of your organization? Would your followers appreciate the chance to greet you? Would these personal interactions remind you that followers are not numbers, assets, or commodities? They are people who have families and dreams...just like you.

All Work and No Fun Leadership

Have you ever worked in an environment where fun was not tolerated? Have you ever had a boss who discouraged socializing with your colleagues because it interferes with getting things done? How did this environment affect you and your colleagues? Did you look forward to going to work or were you counting down the days until you could retire or get a new job?

Having fun while at work can improve the productivity and efficiency of employees as studies have shown.[26] Some companies, such as Warby Parker, even ask their employees to rate their happiness each week on a scale of 1 to 10. As with anything, though, even fun can be overdone. Researchers have also confirmed that a deliberate effort to create fun in the workplace has led to dissatisfied employees.[27] Given the conflicting results of workplace fun, which environment would you thrive in...one that allows you and others to be yourself or

---

[26] Harter, J., Schmidt, F., Asplund, J., Killham, E., & Agrawal, S. (n.d.). Causal impact of employee work perceptions on the bottom line of organizations. *Perspectives on Psychological Science,* 378-389.

[27] Burkeman, O. Who goes to work to have fun? *New York Times,* December 11, 2013.

one that suppresses anything not related to work?

A boss was frustrated with employees because of their constant laughter and banter among themselves as well as their customers. To this boss, this meant that employees were more interested in goofing off than ensuring the work they did was up to standards. In addition, the boss could not concentrate on reviewing things because of the constant giggling and banter of the employees. To address this issue, the boss sent an email setting the following expectations for employees:

- Employees are to reduce the level of laughter and social time with each other as well as customers.
- There will be no more discussing how a work-related telephone call plays out because whether it was funny or frustrating simply is a waste of work time.
- Everyone will have to turn in their completed work for the day to the boss so it can be checked for errors as well as to determine if anyone has time to laugh, socialize, and/or giggle for long stretches of time.
- Errors are not acceptable and will not be tolerated.

How would you react if you received an email containing these workplace expectations? Clearly, the boss is sending a message that fun

in the workplace will not be tolerated. Contrast that with Google, the

#1 rated place to work in 2015, according to Forbes Magazine's

employee survey results. In fact, 90 percent of Google's employees find

their workplace to be fun, and 98 percent of all employees are proud to

say Google is their employer.[28]

There are certainly times in any workplace where fun has to be set

aside to properly accomplish the mission. People who enjoy their jobs

recognize this just as quickly as people who don't. Still, how can you

ignore the Forbes' survey results at Google? With an average of 21

percent of your total lifetime waking hours spent at work, why

shouldn't we at least try to have some fun while we are there?[29]

---

[28] Unknown Author (2015). Fortune's 100 best places to work, Fortune, 2015.
Retrieved October 26, 2015, from
http://reviews.greatplacetowork.com/google-inc

[29] Unknown Author (2012). What percentage of your life will you spend at
work. *RealsSociology*, March 31, 2012. Retrieved October 26, 2015, from
www.realsociology.edublogs.org/2012/03/31/what-percentage-of-your-life-
will-you-spend-at-work/

Failure Is Not an Option for Leaders, But Should

It Be?

Before you went to sleep last night, did you set an alarm clock to make sure you would wake up at a certain time? Once you woke up, did you plan on making coffee and/or eating some breakfast? When you drove or rode in to work, did you start thinking about things you needed to do that day? At what point in the day did you plan to fail at something?

We associate the word failure with negativity, but is that proper? For example, why do we, as leaders, allow ourselves to get frustrated when our followers fail? If you were to go back in your career, could you remember a time where you failed at something? Did you recover from the failure? Did you learn a valuable lesson from failing? Where would you be in your career if you had never failed?

Thomas Edison was a legendary U.S. inventor and credited with inventing the light bulb among other things. A cohort once approached Edison, eager to tell Edison he was a failure because of Edison's reportedly one thousand attempts to create the electric light bulb. When Edison heard the critique, he responded in the contrary. Edison understood the importance of failure and made the argument that his efforts had been quite successful in that he had figured out a thousand ways to invent an electric light bulb that would not work.

Failures are not a direct reflection of our leadership abilities. Failure is an opportunity to learn. How many of you warned your child not to touch a hot burner on the stove? How many of your children did so even after you warned them? Did said child ever touch a hot burner again? While there are certainly times when leaders simply cannot allow their followers to fail, there are also many times when leaders intercede unnecessarily. As you look back on failures in your career, would you have preferred your leader to intercede or would you rather have learned an important lesson from your failure?

Leaders normally have good intentions when they try to assist their followers in their growth by preventing failure. Followers, in turn, normally do not want to fail their leaders. The next time you are confronted with a follower's failure, repress the urge to get frustrated. When you see a situation where a follower is destined to fail but no harm will be done to others, determine if it would be best to facilitate a

lesson learned. Failure is normally not scheduled or planned, but it is

inevitable and, if we allow it, failure can teach us lessons we will never

forget.

The Dangers of Leading While Operating on Automatic Pilot

Have you ever had a leader who seemed to be going through the motions doing only what it takes to get by? If you have endured a leader such as this, did you make a promise to never become that person? How do you think the leader fell into this rut? Was it lack of challenges? Could it be lack of desire? Is it possible that he/she just became stale in the position? Most important, how can you avoid being a leader who operates on automatic pilot?

We have all set and attained goals in our careers. Most of the time, we celebrated our accomplishments and set new goals. Yet despite our aspirations, we fall into ruts where we fall into routines and end up doing things because that's the way we have always done them. These are formidable traps for leaders.

An experiment was created to see how nurses would respond to orders given by people in positions of power, in this case a doctor. In the experiment, the nurses would receive a telephone call from a doctor they had never met and be told to administer a prescribed dose of

medication to a patient on their floor. Normal procedure would be for

the nurses to walk to a dispensary, retrieve the medication, measure

out the prescribed dosage and then proceed to the patient's room and

inject the patient. The designers of the experiment built in conditions

to determine how willing the nurses would be to go against the person

who has perceived authority. As such, the doctor prescribed a 20mg

dose of a certain medication. When nurses went to retrieve the

medication, they would clearly see a message on the box containing the

medication, which read, "Any dose of this medication over 10 mg is

lethal." Out of 22 nurses called, how many of them were on their way

to administer the lethal 20 mg dose of medication to their patient

before experiment administrators stopped them? Would it surprise you

that the experimenters had to stop 21 out of 22 nurses from

administering the lethal dose?[30]

When leaders operate on automatic pilot, we tend to look for the

path of least resistance, which isn't always necessarily the best way to

---

[30] McLeod, S. (2008). Hofling's hospital experiment. *Simply Psychology*.
Retrieved November 11, 2015, from http://www.simplypsychology.org/hofling-obedience.html

go. Would you rather stagnate in your current position or would you rather look for opportunities to grow? Are you, as a leader, committed to challenging your followers every chance you get or would you rather your followers do the same things over and over so it doesn't cause you any extra work? According to the Center for Creative Leadership, 70 percent of executives learned their most valuable leadership lessons from challenging assignments.[31] Falling into the routine is easy, but if you were a follower, would you want your leader to make you think or would you rather your leader act like a zombie operating on automatic pilot?

---

[31] McCarthy, D. (July 25, 2013). Leadership development "Moneyball" | SmartBlogs. Retrieved November 12, 2015, from http://smartblogs.com/leadership/2013/07/25/leadership-development-moneyball/

Leading With Eyes Wide Open: How Our Implicit Biases Blind Us

When you see a spider, do you have a reaction? What about if you are standing on the edge of a platform looking down at a drop of over 1,000 feet? Are there certain kinds of foods that just gross you out as soon as you see or smell them? What about when you are walking down the street? Have you ever seen someone who just made you nervous but you weren't sure why?

All of these feelings are built in to our psyches based on events that have occurred in our lives. Whether you knew it or not, local, regional, and world events, the views espoused by people around you, as well as your life experiences helped shape you to be the person you are today. This is why some people see risk in certain areas while others see reward.

If you have access to the Internet, a magazine, a newspaper, or you are in a public place, we can do a little test. Find three to five different faces in the media in which you have access. When you look at these faces, write down two or three words that come to mind when you first glance at them. Chances are your responses would not match others who also participated in this exercise. This is because we all see things from our perspective.

If you look at the words you wrote down, how likely are you to accurately assess these people? Most of you probably labeled these people based on an instant judgment, but where did our judgments come from? Our minds are constantly working in ways we are not consciously aware. For example, if you are driving in your car and someone swerves into your lane, did you stop to think about moving out of the way or did your mind instinctively activate your muscles to move the car to safety?

This kind of automatic thinking can be valuable as well as dangerous to leaders. While we would instantly judge someone coming at us with a knife as dangerous, we also make similar unconscious decisions regarding those who don't immediately or necessarily represent danger. The latter scenario is where our implicit biases are activated without us knowing they are affecting our decision making.

A television pundit was discussing a very controversial topic on a talk show. She was intelligently arguing her position with other panel members when a statistic from a major newspaper was quoted as a counterpoint to her argument. The pundit was shocked by the statistic because it negated her entire argument. Instead of acknowledging the statistic was damaging, she immediately insisted that the statistic was factually incorrect. When the panel member cited other award-winning investigative stories reported by this same newspaper, the pundit immediately dismissed the contradiction as well as the corresponding statistics because the facts did not fit what she had to say. In this instance, her implicit biases were manifesting in front of her audience when she repeatedly refused to even consider the possibility that her position may, in fact, be incorrect.

Implicit biases affect each of us in similar ways almost every day. Because implicit biases are based in the subconscious, it is difficult for us to even be aware they exist. When we make decisions as leaders, we are typically trying to do what's right, but is it possible our implicit biases unconsciously impact our decision making? Have you ever made a decision as a leader and then looked back at it later wondering how you ever came to that conclusion?

To overcome our implicit biases, we first need to be aware they exist. Research has suggested that if we, as leaders, take more time in the decision-making process, expose ourselves to counter-typical associations, engage in deliberative processing, and seek other perspectives, we may be able to overcome many of our implicit biases.[32] In addition, a devil's advocate may also help to give you a perspective, which your implicit biases may have kept you from considering.

As leaders, we make decisions frequently and many things that have occurred in our lives govern these decisions. Implicit biases exist in all of us and are working on a subconscious level, steering us to certain decisions that although we may think are fair or correct, the opposite can be true. While we are sometimes governed by our blind spots, our followers may have a clear view, which will impact our trust and credibility as a leader. Do you want to continue driving blind or do you want to lead with eyes wide open?

---

[32] Kang, J., Bennett, M., Carbado, D., Casey, P., Dasgupta, N., Faigman, D., Mnookin, J. (November 5, 2012). Implicit bias in the courtroom. *UCLA Law Review*. Retrieved November 13, 2015, from http://www.uclalawreview.org/implicit-bias-in-the-courtroom-2/

The Power of a "Job Well Done"

What kind of leader brings out the best in you? Is it someone who believes in you? Do you like having a leader who openly appreciates how hard you work for the organization? Could a leader who strives to assist in your personal development be one you enjoy serving? Why does it seem there are so few of these types of leaders in today's workforce?

Leaders have a substantial impact on organizational culture and employee motivation. If any of you have ever served under a toxic boss or been part of a toxic culture, you know how stressful it can be. Many people will blame the job for the stress and, in part, they are correct. According to the Whitehall Studies, however, the stress at work is derived from the difference between expended effort and perceived reward.[33] With a toxic culture or a toxic boss, there is little perceived reward. Combine that with high effort and high demands, the

---

[33] Kuper, H., Sing-Manoux, A., Siegrist, J., Marmot, M. (April 26, 2002). When Reciprocity Fails: Effort-Reward Imbalance in Relation to Coronary Heart Disease and Health Functioning in the Whitehall II Study. Occupational and Environmental Medicine. Retrieved April 14, 2016, from http://oem.bmj.com/content/59/11/777.full

environment is a bubbling cauldron of stress, anger, and unhappiness.

Some bosses thrive in this environment, believing that if employees are uncomfortable, work efficiency and productiveness increase. Compliments, according to these bosses, directly lead to employees doing less work because their egos get in the way. One leader even openly characterized his approach to employee motivation as a rabid dog chasing after someone; if the employee knows the boss is right on their tail, the employee will work that much harder to keep the boss at bay. Would that kind of approach from a leader motivate you? Studies have shown that overuse of discipline and creating an environment of fear sabotages worker productivity in that followers are inclined only to do what they know won't get them in trouble.[34]

A police investigator in the field was called to a potential crime scene because of his subject-matter expertise. As this investigator surveyed the scene, he came across something he had never seen before. After carefully looking over the material, he recalled a recent training and concluded the substance to be extremely toxic. When the

---

[34] Michael, M., Gittel, J., & Ledeen, M. (December 1, 2004). Leadership and the fear factor. *MIT Sloan Management Review*. Retrieved November 14, 2015, from http://sloanreview.mit.edu/article/leadership-and-the-fear-factor/

investigator told his leader about his assumption and the basis for it, the leader looked warily at the investigator. The necessary response would require a significant financial outlay to bring an internationally recognized expert to the scene. When the leader agreed to pay to bring the expert to the scene, the leader looked at the investigator and said, "You had better be right on this or you can expect to be transferred."

When the expert arrived, he went into the area where the substance was located and performed tests to confirm the chemical profile. The positive test confirmed that this was the first time the substance had ever been found in the United States. The investigator's intuition and knowledge had helped save the lives of hundreds of people. The expert was impressed and went to the leader to express his admiration for the investigator who tentatively identified the substance. Upon hearing the congratulatory words, the leader looked at the investigator and stated, "Well at least he's smart enough to know when he's in over his head." The leader then abruptly walked off.

True leaders understand the power of their words and actions. Imagine how this follower felt, when after saving hundreds of lives based on recognizing a substance that had yet to be found in the United

States, the leader openly dismissed him and his efforts. Opportunities to praise and show appreciation to your followers are moments where leaders can cement their social bonds. Can you recall times where you missed those opportunities? Do you want to be the leader who nips at their followers' heels trying to scare or threaten them into compliance, or would you prefer to be one of the leaders whose followers give their best efforts because they know their leader appreciates the "job well done"?

Leading With Memorable Messages

Are you as good a communicator as you believe yourself to be? Do your messages resonate with your followers? Do you have a knack for taking complex information and turning it into simpler terms? Do people have a tendency to remember what you say? If you answered yes to these questions, then you have probably never openly wondered why your followers failed to accurately follow your directions.

When we communicate, we believe our words and instructions are perfectly clear and easy for everyone to understand. However, communication is at least a two-party interaction. It involves one person delivering a message and another receiving said message.

You may have participated in some version of a practical exercise commonly referred to as the telephone game. This exercise involves an instructor giving a message to one person in the room and then having individuals repeat the message until it gets to the last person in the room. When the last person to hear the message reveals it aloud, it often has nothing in common with the first message given by the instructor. If we apply this to organizations, imagine what happens to the leader's message as he/she delivers it to one level of managers who then deliver to another level and this layered communication continues until it reaches front-line personnel. What are the chances the leader's message is anywhere near what was intended?

Some would argue digital communication via email and texts allows for leaders to directly communicate with all personnel in the organization. In this manner, the message is delivered directly so there is little chance the message can be distorted. Experience has shown on numerous occasions how context and feelings do not always translate to the digital form.

So at this point, let's perform another test and see how you do. Directly below, you are going to read a slogan and you should try to associate a name with the slogan:

Just Do It _____

Finger Licking Good _____

What Happens Here, Stays Here _____

Breakfast of Champions _____

Eat More Ice Cream!

Where's The Beef? _____

Tastes Great; Less Filling _____

So how did you do? Did you recognize the slogans of Nike, Kentucky Fried Chicken, Las Vegas, Wheaties, Wendy's and Miller Lite? Good for you if you did. Now can you repeat the first sentence in this article? What? You're having trouble? This fact is not surprising.

Some of you will claim that you have heard these slogans over and over again and that is why they have stuck in your mind. When was the last time you heard the slogan, "Where's the beef?" and "Tastes great; less filling?" These ads were aired in 1984 and 1994-1996 respectively. You haven't heard these slogans in 20 or 30 years, and you still remember them today.

Authors Dan and Chip Heath wrote, *Made to Stick: Why Some Ideas Survive and Others Die*. The authors argue that for a message to stick, the message needs to be simple, unexpected, concrete, credible, emotional, and in the form of a story (SUCCES model).[35] If you look at the slogans above, you can see the messages are simple in that they

---

[35] Heath, C., & Heath, D. (2007). *Made to stick: Why some ideas survive and others die*. New York: Random House.

don't contain extraneous words, unexpected or contradicting against accepted beliefs (Tastes great; less filling), concrete in the form of evoking imagery (Finger licking good), credible in that they augment expected beliefs (Breakfast of champions), drawing on people's emotions (Where's the beef) and in the form of telling stories (What happens in Vegas, stays in Vegas). Could we increase retention of our messages by followers if we adapted to include facets of the SUCCES model in our delivery?

The Heaths coin a term in their book called the "curse of knowledge," which means that when we communicate, we know exactly what message we are trying to convey. We choose our words and expect everyone to perceive them as we intended. Experience has shown us that sometimes people take our words out of context or associate them with different meanings. Other times, people just naturally don't pay as much attention as they should. Instead of blaming others for not listening, maybe we should be looking within to ensure we have indeed crafted a memorable message. Now, can you repeat the first sentence in this chapter?

Lincoln's 2nd Rule of Leadership

When you direct a follower to do something and the follower chooses to ignore said direction, how do you feel as the leader? Are you disappointed and/or angry? What if this same follower ignored your direction a second time? Would your reaction change? Would you be angrier? What if you went to question this follower and the follower deliberately dismissed you? Would you be upset? Are you inclined to discipline this person? President Lincoln was, but when presented with this situation, he did things and reacted in ways most of us would not expect.

On November 13, 1861, President Lincoln traveled to General George McClellan's home accompanied by Secretary of State John Seward and Presidential Secretary John Hay. When they arrived, McClellan was out, so they waited inside McClellan's home. McClellan had returned home shortly after Lincoln had arrived, but instead of greeting Lincoln, McClellan chose to ignore Lincoln and went to bed. Further, McClellan instructed his porter to wait 30 minutes before advising President Lincoln of McClellan's declination to meet with the group. Upon leaving, Hay was extremely upset and inquired if the President felt the same way. Lincoln calmly responded by saying, "Better at this time not to be making points of etiquette and personal dignity."[36]

At the time of the personal indignation, Lincoln still believed McClellan to be the best general to lead the Union forces. Although Lincoln intentionally never returned to McClellan's home, he did not let personal judgment get in the way of a practical decision, so Lincoln allowed McClellan to retain his position. Eventually Lincoln lost confidence in McClellan, and in March 1962, McClellan was relieved of his duties.

As soon as McClellan was disciplined, Lincoln instructed one of his advisors to immediately visit McClellan. The advisor was surprised by Lincoln's directive. When the advisor inquired as to the purpose of the McClellan visit, Lincoln stressed the importance of rebuilding McClellan's personal confidence. The directive surprised the advisor inasmuch as President Lincoln had just fired McClellan. Lincoln, sensing

---

[36] Retrieved July 6, 2015, from http://www.history.com/this-day-in-history/mcclellan-snubs-lincoln

the confusion, explained his directive by telling the advisor that General McClellan, even though he failed in this moment, still had skills that could prove useful to the Union in the future. President Lincoln wanted McClellan to be ready if it was necessary to utilize his skills.

How many of us could have ignored the personal slights and the open insubordination? How many of us would have felt a compelling urge to prove to McClellan who was the boss? How many of us would have written McClellan off forever? How many of us, consciously or unconsciously, put our needs ahead of our followers?

President Lincoln was able to set aside personal feelings and recognize value in people regardless of how they felt about him or chose to treat him. To Lincoln, the union's preservation was his first priority. As we evaluate ourselves, do we allow our needs to take priority or do we take the view of Lincoln and try to find value in people even when they don't necessarily deserve it?

Getting Under Your Skin

Has anyone ever said something to you that just made you mad? How did you react to that person? Did you respond in kind immediately hurling an insult in their direction? Maybe you suppressed it, but you probably did plenty of venting at a later appropriate time. It may even be likely that you went to confront that person and give them a piece of your mind. If you did these things, did you consider the possibility that this is the exact behavior that person wanted?

We are all subject to emotional hijackings wherein something said or done to us causes us to react in certain ways. The events that cause these hijackings are referred to as triggers. When the hijackings occur, our emotions are let loose and we sometimes do or say things we regret later. Is it possible for us to control our reaction when our emotional triggers are ignited?

A part of emotional intelligence is self-regulation, wherein we are able to recognize we are experiencing emotion and attempt to regulate it before we get to the point of regret. You will probably agree that it is easier said than done. If you are able to self-regulate in these situations, however, there are important benefits.

As you can imagine, people being arrested are not typically happy with what is occurring. This serves as an emotional trigger to them and many of them lash out in anger by insulting the arresting officers. There are frequent references to manhood (or lack thereof), derogatory familial references, as well as the inability to attract loved ones due to a lack of beauty. One such arrestee was very creative in his insults by stringing together a series of four letter words in a unique but artistic way to get his point across. With such personally directed insults, it would have been easy for team members to fall victim to the trigger and be emotionally hijacked. Instead, team members looked at the arrestee and asked him if he couldn't come up with something better. Another team member followed with his own creative string of four letter words. For a few long seconds, the arrestee looked at the team members before he bowed his head. Arrest team members had shown that his vile words would not set off their trigger, which, not getting the response he expected or desired, caused the arrestee to be silent for the remainder of the trip to jail.

When people try to trigger an emotional response, they are

seeking to hold power over you. By getting you mad and getting you to respond angrily, you are effectively catering to their needs. If you are able to self-regulate and stop the emotional hijacking, you effectively take all power away from them. As a leader, how would your followers feel if they saw you self-regulate in a situation that did not necessarily call for an emotional response? Would you be setting the tone for them to follow? It is important to remember as a leader that no one makes you mad. Rather, you make yourself mad.[37]

---

[37] Tavris, C., & Aronson, E. (2007). *Mistakes were made (but not by me): Why we justify foolish beliefs, bad decisions, and hurtful acts*. Orlando, FL.: Harcourt.

How a Simple Telephone Call Changed a Culture

When is the last time you told your followers how much you appreciate them? Has it been a while since you offered a follower an unsolicited compliment? Can you recall the last time one of your leaders came to you and recognized the work you have been doing for your organization? Does being noticed by a leader have an impact on workplace performance, satisfaction, attitude, and/or engagement?

On average, most of us work around 2,000 hours per year. Much of the time, the only people who notice what we do at work are our immediate supervisors. Many executives will argue that employees are the most valuable assets of any organization but these same people rarely acknowledge them among their peers.

Gallup conducted a study on employee motivation and found that 50 percent of current employees are not engaged at work and an additional 20 percent are actively disengaged. Do these percentages reflect your employee engagement? If so, what are you doing as the leader to re-engage your followers? How can you increase their motivation?

The common assumption is that employees are motivated by money. However, this is often incorrect. If a person makes a living wage, money as a motivator becomes increasingly less important. What followers and fellow employees need to stoke their intrinsic motivation is positive affirmation from their leader.

A leader of a government agency found many followers in the organization to be actively disengaged. Previous leaders had taken followers' work for granted. What resulted was an unmotivated workforce. The new leader had a desire to be a transformational leader so he endeavored to establish a connection to all of the followers in the organization. This leader immediately established a program where he would be notified of successes in all offices under his purview. At least once a week, the leader took time out of his day and telephonically contacted the people instrumental in the successes reported to him. In the call, he would congratulate the follower on their accomplishment, acknowledge their effort, and commend them for doing a great job.

These telephone calls became a badge of honor to the recipients. The leader had not only taken the time to contact them, the leader also praised their efforts. Word of these phone calls from the leader quickly spread to every person in the office. All of a sudden, people who thought they were anonymous to executives transformed into engaged employees who took pride in working together as a team to accomplish the agency mission. Intrinsic motivation levels increased throughout the organization within a short time. To this day, the leader still makes these telephone calls at least once per week.

Employee disengagement causes immense financial losses in organizations due to lost productivity. Leaders as well as managers frequently misdiagnose the problem laying the lack of motivation at the feet of employees instead of self-assessing to determine what they can do differently. Corporations trying to get people re-engaged at work have spent millions of dollars in an attempt to solve the issue. Instead of spending money, maybe leaders should instead take the time to tell their followers, "Great job!"

What's Up With Generation Y? Baby Boomer's and Generation X's Frustration in Leading the New Generation

Statistics show Generation Y members are the most technically savvy generation as well as the most educated but also the most narcissistic. As leaders from a different generation, we can easily become frustrated with Generation Y. Members of this generation constantly ask why they are being told to do something instead of just doing what they were told. How often have you heard people complain about how Generation Y members are not as dedicated to the profession as previous generations? Why do Baby Boomers and Generation X members frequently complain about how Generation Y members are not willing to stay late to accomplish the mission but instead putting a social gathering before an important work task? As frustrated as Generation X and Baby Boomers get, is Generation Y's behavior necessarily a bad thing?

When you first started in your organization, were there occasions where leaders assured you that family came before work? How did you feel when you heard those statements? Did they reassure you? Did you feel like the employer cared about you? Even if they did or didn't, let's try to self-assess. Have we followed through on that commitment to family? If you're a Baby Boomer or Generation X, how many birthdays, anniversaries, recitals, and other family events have you missed because of work? Members of Generation Y also can ask that question, but the odds say they will have a much different answer than the Baby Boomer and Generation X members.

Generation Y members refuse to miss important family and social events. To them, friends and family are much more important than any job tasks. This is a source of frustration for Baby Boomers and Generation X members because they have traditionally stayed at work to complete whatever work was needed. Generation Y members' reputation suffered because of these acts, and they are frequently described as entitled and only about themselves. Are those allegations accurate?

Police officers frequently are asked to work off-duty security details at various private enterprises. Baby Boomers and Generation X members frequently took as many of these off-duty assignments as they could get so that they could earn extra income for their families. In their minds, they sacrificed so their family could benefit.

Speaking with supervisors in police organizations today, they lament the fact that they cannot get people to volunteer for these off-duty events and frequently have to assign someone to it. Generation Y has been revealing how different they are from Baby Boomers and Generation X in their refusals. Just because Generation Y members look at things differently, does that make them wrong? If Generation Y members get on your nerves, ask yourself who helped to create them? Who told Generation Y they could be anything they wanted to be? Did any of you tell them that family comes before work? So why are you now surprised that Generation Y is the first generation to actually believe it?

Listen = Silent: Why Great Leaders Pay Attention to Followers

Don't you hate it when you are speaking with people and when their cell phone rings, they immediately answer, leaving your conversation in limbo? What about when their phone jingles and they can't wait to put their phone up to their face so they can read their new text message? How do you feel when you're at work talking to someone sitting behind their desk and you catch them furtively glancing out of the corner of their eye monitoring their email and instant messaging? What if the person who did these things was your leader?

More and more, leadership is about establishing relationships with followers built on mutual trust. Can a leader possibly earn someone's trust when the person is talking but the leader is more engrossed in an email or text? How many times have you been in a conversation when the other party didn't hear a word you said because of their attention to a message on an electronic device? Earning trust, however, is harder than it seems. Sometimes, a leader has to make the first move.

In his book, *It's Your Ship*, Admiral D. Michael Abrashoff researched why USS Benfold crew members did not reenlist. One of their complaints was that they felt disrespected and that no one would listen to them. Admiral Abrashoff found the time to meet or have personal conversations with every member of his crew using these meetings and conversations to determine how to make the work culture better. While many bosses have had similar conversations with employees, Abrashoff showed that not only had he listened, he took action to incorporate some of their suggestions. This and other leadership techniques helped Abrashoff and his crew turn the USS Benfold from the worst ship to the best ship in the U.S. Navy.[38]

If we contrast Abrashoff's story with another leader, you can see a stark difference. This leader enjoyed the reputation of being one of the nicest people to work for in the office. In an annual review, the leader reviewed current cases with a follower who advised that one particular case had no merit. A few days later, the leader, walking down the hall with a member of executive management, openly praised the meritless case. Later, the follower went to the leader and reminded the leader

---

[38] Abrashoff, D. M. (2002). *It's your ship: Management techniques from the best damn ship in the Navy*. New York, NY: Warner.

that the case was going nowhere. The leader acknowledged the follower and apologized only to make the same statement a week later.

When people perceive leaders aren't listening, it devalues followers' input. Instead of being seen as an integral member of a team, followers can see themselves as cogs in a machine. Are you more inspired by a leader who doesn't listen to you or one who values your opinion and engages you in conversation? If you rearrange the letters L-I-S-T-E-N, you can spell S-I-L-E-N-T, which is a tool all leaders can use to generate trust with their followers.

Swimming With Sharks: How to Lead in a Toxic Culture

Have you ever had an occasion where from the moment you walked into the workplace, you knew there were problems? Do you remember encountering employees who, no matter what their leader did, were never pleased or happy with anything? Are you in an environment where everyone seems to continually focus on the negative aspects instead of the positive? What would you do if you were a leader in a toxic culture?

So many people have posited that changing a culture is not an easy thing to do. Maybe not, but there have been numerous stories told where such change did not involve a lengthy drawn out battle between those for and against change. Sometimes all it took was getting the right leader in place.

Jim Collins, author of *Good to Great*, argues that getting the right people on the bus and the wrong people off the bus is the first priority for change. Collins tells the story of Fannie Mae and its CEO named

David Maxwell. The organization was losing significant amounts of money when Maxwell took over and he followed Collins' advice by bringing in his managers, setting his expectations, and telling the managers that if they didn't think or they didn't want to keep up with Maxwell's demands, it was probably best if they were to get off the bus. Fourteen of 26 managers left Fannie Mae after their conversations with Maxwell.[39]

Sometimes, especially in public sector employment, you don't have the opportunity to get the wrong people off the bus, which leaves us with the dilemma of what to do with toxic employees? Should we transfer them? Should we ignore them? Should we just bide our time biting our lips in frustration until someone moves on to a different position or quits the organization? Are these the actions of a true leader?

Another thing to consider is how does the toxic employee affect followers? Scientific studies show that emotions are contagious. If a leader is not careful, toxicity can quickly evolve into a viral infection spreading throughout an organization. Can you promote quick enough

---

[39] Collins, J. (2001). *Good to great: Why some companies make the leap – and others don't.* New York, NY: HarperBusiness.

to avoid the ramifications of such an outbreak?

In 1914, Admiral Ernest Shackleton led a group of explorers whose goal was to be the first men to traverse Antarctica. Shackleton's ship eventually was frozen and stuck in an ice floe. The men spent approximately 2 years on the ice floe as they watched the ice destroy their ship and fought the battle to survive in harsh conditions. As you can imagine, pessimism, anger, and panic were always bubbling just below the surface, ready to take over sanity and the patience needed to survive. Shackleton always served as a beacon of hope but was smart enough to know who his toxic sailors were. When it came time to organize a crew to attempt to sail a small lifeboat across an open sea to try to reach help, whom do you think Shackleton chose as his crew?

If you answered the most toxic sailors, you would be correct. Shackleton understood that if he left these sailors behind, their negativity would take over and cause the demise of all who remained behind. Shackleton knew that if these sailors were with him, he would be able to continue his optimism and mitigate the damage they could do to others. Shackleton and his group of toxic sailors finally made it to Elephant Island in April 1916 and were able to use another ship to rescue the remaining crew members in August 1916. Every one of

Shackleton's sailors made it home alive and well.[40] What do you think

would have happened if Shackleton had left his most toxic sailors

behind with the rest of the group? Would there have been anyone left

alive to rescue?

Toxic employees are in every organization. If left unchecked,

their attitudes can become a cancer, infecting every person who comes

in contact with them. The easier path is to find a way to cut them out of

the organization but there are times when a surgical removal is not

possible. It is in these moments that followers look to their leaders for

help just as the sailors did with Shackleton on the long cold days and

nights. No one wants to work in a negative environment where people

collect grievances as often as they breathe. What steps are you taking

as a leader to protect your people from the cloud of negativity

generated by toxic employees?

---

[40] Koehn, N. F. (2011). Leadership Lessons From the Shackleton Expedition. *New York Times*, December 24, 2011. Retrieved August 9, 2015, from http://www.nytimes.com/2011/12/25/business/leadership-lessons-from-the-shackleton-expedition.html

A Leadership Bucket List

Remember when you were just starting out in your chosen career? Do you remember the excitement? Finally, you were getting the chance to showcase your skills, make a difference, and earn a little money while you were at it. You may have even made a mental or written list of goals and objectives for your career. If you can recall that list or if you still have it, how many goals and objectives have you accomplished?

During the past week, I saw a young man, probably still in college, composing a list of things he wanted to do before he died, his bucket list if you will. The list contained the normal entries. He wanted to see sights such as the Northern Lights, visit all 50 U.S. states and travel to every country in the world. He hoped to get married some day and to have children. He also wanted to find his dream job, make a good living and retire early. Sound somewhat familiar?

If we think back, our goals and objectives when starting our careers probably weren't that different from the young man. Like all of us, there were certain things we hoped to accomplish before the end of our career. Maybe most of us have accomplished what we set out to do.

But if we were to look back and reassess our original goals and objectives, would we be happy with them?

Now come back to where you are today in your career. Create a new list of goals and objectives. Compare these with the goals and objectives you had in your past. Are they similar or are they very different? If they are different, ask yourself why? Has experience changed your perspective? Were your initial goals and objectives skewed towards self-aggrandizement over the betterment of others? Did accomplishment involve individual notoriety or societal improvement?

When I saw the young man making his bucket list, I wanted to stop him and offer advice like I had received on my first day with the FBI. However, as with me in my earlier years, young ears don't always hear. On that first night at the FBI Academy, an old, grizzled veteran agent told us that in a few months, we would walk out of the FBI Academy with an FBI badge and credentials and as soon as we showed our ID, we would be granted instantaneous respect, none of which was earned. The advice he gave next was the best career goal I have ever gotten and one that was missing from the young man's bucket list. Simply put, his directive was to leave the place better than you found it. Can you meet

that goal and if so, imagine what kind of legacy you could leave as a

leader?

The Leadership Legacy Tree

In your organization, are you expected to meet certain goals or objectives? Is your performance measured by company metrics to define success? Do you go through quarterly, semiannual, or annual reviews where your performance and career trajectory are discussed? With so many performance measures being objectively quantified, how can we measure leadership?

There are plenty of arguments supporting the idea of economic indicators as a measure of leadership. In the world of business and government, acronyms such as ROI (Return on Investment), GDP (Gross Domestic Product), and CPI (Consumer Price Index) are common terms tossed around to measure production, efficiency, and progress. In theory, these performance metrics are directly related to the performance and success of the leader. History has shown us, however, that just because someone was able to achieve high performance metrics does not necessarily mean they are successful leaders.

In the National Football League (NFL), an American professional sports league, there are iconic coaches whose names continue to be heard even though they are deceased or no longer hold coaching positions in the league. Names like Bill Walsh, Tom Landry, and Bill Parcells are iconic because they mentored a number of people who went on to their own successful careers in the NFL.

NFL aficionados have coined the term "coaching tree" when referencing these and other coaches. To illustrate this concept, a family tree style diagram was used. The coach being discussed was pictured on the trunk of the tree and each branch represented an assistant coach who moved on to become an NFL head coach. Limbs then grew from the branches, representing other assistant coaches who developed into NFL coaches after learning from the understudy. The coaching trees of Walsh, Landry and Parcells were full and dense with branches and limbs going in every direction. Could a similar tree diagram be used to measure our leadership by using branches and limbs to show how many leaders we have helped to create?

The legacy you leave in the future is dependent on the steps you take today. As you lead, are you challenging your followers or maintaining the status quo? Are you collaborating or micromanaging? Are you mentoring or are you dictating? Are you focusing on organizational metrics or are you focusing on preparing your followers

for the future?

Not too long ago, a leader in one organization was asked to

interview for a job with a new company. One of the questions asked by

the hiring committee was what would happen to his old department if

he left his position. His reply…"Absolutely nothing." This leader had

established his leadership legacy tree by preparing his followers to take

his place and be leaders in their own right. If you left your organization

tomorrow, what would your leadership legacy tree look like?

The Top 10 Percent: How Overconfidence Can

Lead to Bad Decisions

Think about all the leaders in your organization, including yourself. If you had to rank leaders in your organization by their effectiveness, would you rate yourself in the upper half or bottom half? Would you go as far to place yourself in the top 20 percent among your peers? Chances are, many of you rated yourself in at least the upper half of effective leaders in your organization. Would you be surprised that most people rank themselves in the upper half of effective leaders in their organizations?

In many situations, we tend to see ourselves in a favorable light. For example, when we do something that hurts someone, we say we were provoked or had no choice. We never say we are a mean person. Likewise, when we do something that benefits someone, we immediately reason we did so because we are nice people.[41] Given that

---

[41] Tavris, C., & Aronson, E. (2007). *Mistakes were made (but not by me): Why we justify foolish beliefs, bad decisions, and hurtful acts*. Orlando, FL: Harcourt.

we are naturally reluctant to be critical of ourselves, we can quickly

grow overconfident in our abilities.

In a study of 44 veteran police officers who averaged 14 years of

investigative experience, participants were asked to watch videotaped

interviews of suspects conducted by an experienced police officer to

determine their guilt or innocence based on their verbal and nonverbal

behavior. All officers expressed almost 100 percent confidence in their

choices, but none of them performed better than chance. What was

also surprising was that two-thirds of the officers who participated in

the study had also attended advanced interview/interrogation training

to include the Reid school. Believing that their experience and training

gave them an edge over untrained people, the police officers mistakenly

grew overconfident in their abilities.[42] Is it possible that our training

and experiences have led us to become overconfident in certain areas

of our lives?

Overconfidence also leads us to stronger convictions in our

---

[42] Tavris, C., & Aronson, E. (2007). *Mistakes were made (but not by me): Why we justify foolish beliefs, bad decisions, and hurtful acts*. Orlando, FL: Harcourt.

abilities to self-assess. Judges pride themselves on being objective in the courtroom and being fair in their decision making. In a study by Jeffrey Rachlinski, Chris Guthrie, and Andrew Wistrich, 35 out of 36 judges (97 percent) surveyed rated themselves in the top quartile of judges when it came to avoiding racial prejudice in decision making. Unfortunately, studies also have proven that when we believe ourselves to be objective, it leads us to be less objective and more susceptible to our implicit biases.[43] Although the judges certainly did not intend to allow bias to affect their decisions, overconfidence in their own ability to be objective ensured it would happen.

We often fail to recognize when overconfidence creeps into our leadership style. The affliction is difficult to notice because there will be plenty of followers willing to speak only the words they think you want to hear. This, in turn, will feed the inner beast of ego and hubris. If unchecked, your leadership journey can quickly become sidetracked, or even worse, abruptly terminated. Guarding against overconfidence is critical to a leader's success. Will you be in the top half of leaders in

---

[43] "Implicit Bias in the Courtroom Jerry Kang UCLA LAW REVIEW ..." Web. 19 Oct. 2015.

your organization who are able to keep their ego in check?

How Important Is Trust

Have you ever had a boss you didn't trust? What impact did that mistrust have on that person's ability to lead? Without any credibility, did this person ever have a chance of being a leader to you? What about the trust between you and your followers? Is it strong like concrete or is it fragile like glass? What are some ways that you can build and increase trust between you and your followers?

Joseph Schafer, a professor at Southern Illinois University, performed a study involving over 1,500 police officers. These officers were asked what they believe is the most important trait of leaders in police organizations. Overwhelmingly, the number one response was that followers needed to be able to trust their leader.[44] Trust is something that doesn't come easy, especially when it comes to law enforcement. In law enforcement as with many other professions, trust must be earned.

---

[44] Schafer, J. (2013). *Effective leadership in policing: Successful traits and habits.* Durham, NC: Carolina Academic Press.

Eat More Ice Cream!

A sheriff in a large Florida county always talked about the importance of gaining and keeping the public trust. In meetings with his leader, this sheriff constantly stressed how he wanted his followers to do the right thing. This sheriff believed that honesty and integrity were the foundation of a good police department. One day, the sheriff was at the county courthouse when he got in his car and pulled out of his parking spot. As he pulled out, he accidentally bumped into another car. The sheriff got out of his car to survey the damage when one of his deputies arrived. The sheriff waited while the deputy filled out the incident report. As the deputy came over to give the sheriff a copy of the report, the deputy advised the sheriff there would be no ticket issued for the infraction. At this point, the sheriff directed the deputy to write a ticket for the infraction. The deputy continued to resist, uncomfortable with the obligation of writing his sheriff a ticket that would cost the sheriff a couple hundred dollars. The sheriff stood his ground until the ticket was issued. As the sheriff left the scene, he reminded his deputy that he deserved the same treatment as any other citizen in the county.

In this instance, would you have insisted on the deputy writing you a ticket that would cost you a significant amount of money? Wouldn't it have been easier just to thank the deputy and let the insurance companies sort out the costs? If the sheriff had chosen that path, what do you think it would have done to the bonds of trust between him and his followers? The next time the sheriff spoke to his followers about honesty and integrity, would they have listened? Would you have chosen to follow that sheriff if he would have foregone the ticket but continued with his promotion of honesty and integrity?

Followers are constantly watching their leaders to see if they will follow the guidelines they expect of others. In addition, they want to know that the leader has their best interests in both mind and action. In this case, the sheriff was able to earn a greater trust with his followers because he promoted honesty and when that moment came for the sheriff to show he truly believed in the value of honesty, the sheriff ensured he would be treated just as he would expect anyone else to be treated. Leaders frequently ask their followers to trust them but leaders must first earn that trust.

The Secret Ways We Are Affected by Priming

Can you influence your followers to take certain actions? Can your followers influence you to make certain decisions? How aware are you of being influenced? Is it possible you could be influenced to make a decision without consciously being aware of it? Would it surprise you to know you are constantly being influenced on both conscious and unconscious levels?

If you watch television, you see a barrage of advertisements. Most of the time, we don't pay attention to them, but they still have an effect. For example, some advertisements have a catchy jingle contained within and even though you don't pay attention, chances are you can sing along to the jingle as soon as you hear the first few notes. This is an example of priming where your mind can be programmed to think in a certain manner.

In a classic study, college students were primed with words such as Florida, bingo, and retired. After being primed, these students were asked to walk down a hallway to another room. Unbeknownst to them, they were being timed as they walked. Students who were primed with words associated with elderly people took a significantly longer time to walk down the hallway than those college students who were not primed. Behavior also can be primed in the workplace.

In a classic legal case referred to as the Christian burial case, police officers had investigated a case involving a missing girl. They eventually developed enough evidence to make an arrest. When police tried to question the individual, he asserted his right to an attorney, which according to law, meant that police could no longer ask the suspect questions without having the suspect's attorney present. As they were riding toward the jail, an officer in the front seat started speaking aloud and opining what might happen to a body if it weren't found for months. Inasmuch as they were in a northern climate, the officer talked about how the cold would affect the body, how animals could find the body, and how the parents of the child wouldn't have peace for many months. The officer ended his soliloquy by stating how nice it would be if the little girl and the family could have the benefit of having a nice Christian burial. After hearing the officer talk, the suspect changed his mind and led the officers to the dead girl's body. Even though the ensuing confession was ruled inadmissible, the suspect spoke up because he had been primed.

Priming can also serve more nefarious purposes as well. A police officer who wore his emotions on his sleeves was primed by his peers with stories about a child molestation case prior to an arrest. His colleagues told graphic stories of the suffering the child endured. Then they told the officer there was no way this criminal was going to give up without a fight. On the day of the arrest, the officer was awash with anger. He wanted to take out his frustrations on the suspect, but luckily a supervisor recognized his hyperintensive state and pulled him back from the arrest team. Later, this officer wondered why he had felt the way he did, and he realized that his colleagues had used his emotions to unknowingly bring him to the brink of a response he would have regretted forever. With that knowledge in hand, the officer learned how to temper those emotions whenever he felt them rising, but some people aren't as self-aware as to when they are being primed. Being unaware of the effects produced by priming can potentially lead to regrettable outcomes.

Words, actions, and exposure to certain images can lead to priming individual behavior. In a leadership class, a student spoke about how putting on SWAT gear primed him to feel aggressive. Leaders who use "I" instead of "we" will have an effect on whether or not their followers perceive themselves to be part of a team. Your emotions prime your followers to respond similarly. If you are skeptical about the effects of priming, check to see if your mouth waters the next time a delicious dessert pops up on your television screen.

Creating Stories: How Information Gaps Affect Leadership

Have you ever been in a conversation with someone where you didn't feel like you were getting the whole story? Has your boss ever walked by and given you a look? Maybe one of your friends didn't let you in on some information causing you to question why they would do so. When this happened, did you come up with a reason why these people did these things? In that moment, what are the chances that your emotions hijack your common sense?

We all know what happens when we assume information to be true, yet we make assumptions every single day of our lives. In communication with others, we make assumptions by not only what was said, but also by what was not said. Sometimes what is not said is the more powerful variable of the two.

When information is lacking or things aren't clearly explained, it is natural for us to come up with a story to fill in the gaps. These stories are based on what we perceived as the truth or the reason why information was given or withheld. For example, an employee aware of upcoming promotions could be seriously affected by whether a boss acknowledges him/her or doesn't acknowledge him/her in a meeting.

Once we have authored a story to fill in the communication gaps, emotions follow. Joy, admiration, sadness and anger can each overwhelm the mind based on what was perceived by the individual. This, in turn, can lead to a response either verbally or physically on some occasions. Have you ever reacted to a situation with one of these or other emotions only to find out later that the information you used to fill the gap was incorrect? How did you feel when you found the correct information? Did you apologize or did you muster a reason to rationalize your assumptions/behavior?

A mid-level leader in a large organization was in direct competition with a colleague for a promotion. As this leader was walking into the police chief's office, his competitor walked out and winked at him. The chief, who was on the phone, motioned for the leader to sit down and as he did so, the leader spotted his personnel file sitting on the chief's desk. Immediately, the leader knew what had happened. His competitor had backstabbed him. The leader felt his anger start to rise. The leader had to get even with his colleague justifying his retaliation with the excuse that the leader didn't start this battle. When the chief got off the telephone, the leader was about to explode with anger but before he could, the chief grabbed the leader's file and congratulated him on his new promotion.

As leaders, we have to understand that people, including ourselves, will create stories to fill in informational gaps. We will not be able to stop this from happening. What we need to realize, however, is that we can stem the damage from these stories by noticing our behavior, self-regulating our own emotions, and maintaining adherence to the facts of the situation.[45] If we can do these things, the untold story will not get in the way of the truth.

---

[45] Patterson, K. (2002). *Crucial conversations: Tools for talking when stakes are high.* New York, NY: McGraw-Hill.

The Dark Side of Authority

Do you recall the corporate scandals of Enron, WorldCom, Tyco, and Bernie Madoff? Multibillion dollar corporations ruined by greed. Why is it that so few people stood up to the executives who coopted their organizations for personal gain? Would you have made a stand protesting the illicit and illegal acts being performed? Are you surprised at how quickly people fall in line with authority? You shouldn't be. Despite what you think, you may not do what you think you would when approached by someone in authority.

Since childhood, we have learned to place an emphasis on authority. We were taught to behave in a classroom, to listen to Mom and Dad, and to defer to police. The idea of obeying authority figures is as ingrained into our psyche as breathing, and this behavior can lead us to do things we couldn't imagine.

A psychologist named Stanley Milgram shocked the world in the 1940s when he devised an experiment to try to explain why so many ordinary people did such extraordinarily heinous acts during the Holocaust. Milgram brought in volunteers to either act as a student or teacher in a hypothetical learning experiment. What the volunteer didn't know was that the selection process was rigged so that the volunteer would automatically be the teacher and the so-called student was just an actor. The student and teacher were separated and the teacher was told that for every incorrect answer given, the teacher would have to administer increasing levels of electric shock to the student. The student intentionally missed questions, which led to the unwitting teacher believing they were administering increasing levels of electric shock. As the level of voltage increased, the teacher heard the student's cries of pain as well as heartfelt pleas by the student actor to stop the experiment. In this instance, some teachers would look to the experimenter, represented by a man wearing a lab coat, and express their reluctance to continue. The experimenter would only say that he would take responsibility and that the experiment needed the teacher to continue. Would you believe that 67 percent of volunteers administered lethal doses of electric shock to students just because a man wearing a lab coat asked them to do so?

What takes years to develop cannot necessarily be undone in a short time. When people are told what to do by a person in a position of authority, the natural inclination is to follow those orders. Leaders who have good hearts and their follower's best interests in mind are easy to follow. What's more difficult is when the person making the decisions asks you to do something that sparks the contrarian voice in your head. Our default behavior when faced with this situation is to obey, but if you were going to be a true leader, would you defy authority or blindly follow instructions?

Do You Like Being Told What to Do? Neither Do Your Followers!

If you were to look at your organizational chart, would you describe it as appropriate to meet the needs of today's world? Does it allow people to make decisions or do they have to seek approval from above? Do your followers feel like they have to come to you before deciding what to do next? Is that what you were forced to do prior to becoming a leader? If you had your choice, would you rather work in a strict command and control organizational structure or would you rather work in an organizational structure that gave you the freedom to make important choices?

In his book *Drive*, Daniel Pink identified three keys to employee motivation: autonomy, mastery, and purpose. The more employees are allowed to make decisions on their own, the more motivated they are.[46] Autonomy encourages followers to take pride in their work, and it also helps build trust between leaders and followers.

---

[46] Pink, D. (2009). *Drive: The surprising truth about what motivates us*. New York, NY: Riverhead Books.

The Ritz-Carlton hotel chain leadership implemented a program that uses a unique approach to customer service. Whenever a customer has a problem at a hotel, every employee is authorized to spend up to $2,000 to fix the problem and/or improve a customer's experience without getting the approval of a manager. Clearly, Ritz-Carlton leadership is telling followers that we trust you will make the best decision for our customers. This mindset is established early on as employees of the Ritz-Carlton are told they have been selected rather than being hired, encouraging employees to believe they are part of a distinct group of people more than capable of practicing good judgment.[47]

On January 25, 2014, Medric Cecil Mills, Jr., suffered a heart attack in a parking lot directly across the street from a Washington, D.C., fire department. People knocked on the fire department's door three times pleading for assistance, but none came. Firefighters told people they could not respond unless they were dispatched. It took almost 15 minutes for an ambulance to arrive, but Mr. Mills eventually died. In an

---

[47] Solomon, M. (October 28, 2013). How Ritz-Carlton and Four Seasons empower employees and ... Retrieved September 6, 2015, from

ensuing Investigation, it was learned that the procedural requirements for the fire department involved notifying the officer in charge who would then decide what action to take.[48]

In our two examples, we have one organization that grants their people the freedom to make choices and in the other, the leader decides what the followers should do. Would you rather your leader tell you what to do or would you rather figure out things on your own? Would Mr. Mills still be alive today had the firefighers walked across the street? Maybe or maybe not, but as leaders, shouldn't we trust and empower our followers to make a decision on their own?

---

[48] Hermann, P. (January 30, 2014). Man, 7, dies after collapsing near D.C. fire station and not getting immediate aid. *The Washington Post*. Retrieved September 6, 2015, from http://www.highbeam.com/doc/1P2-35646124.html?

Michael Bret Hood

Walking the Walk

Are leaders supposed to walk the walk and talk the talk? Have you
ever seen someone who claims to be a leader say something and then
do the exact opposite? What was your reaction when you were given a
standard that people higher than you in the organization didn't have to
follow? How did this situation affect their leadership status, assuming
they ever had any in the first place?

In the book, *The New Psychology of Leadership: Identity, Influence
and Power*, the authors assert that for people to be leaders, they need
to be the in-group prototype among other things.[49] This means that
followers see the leader as the best person to represent the goals of the
group. Leaders must continually show they have the followers' best
interests in mind and will tend to their needs. Where leaders get in
trouble is if they start to create a separation between what is asked of
the group and what the leader does.

For example, an organization required quarterly training for all

---

[49] Haslam, S., & Reicher, S. (2011). *The new psychology of leadership identity,
influence, and power*. Hove, England: Psychology Press.

employees. The training, although beneficial, quickly became routine

and repetitive, causing some people to dread going. Executive leaders

were no different. As the quarterly trainings progressed, executive

leaders became noticeably absent from the trainings. On other

occasions when they did attend, they were disruptive in the class while

laughing and joking about the requirements or simply signed the

training log and left without attending. Their followers were not

allowed to do any of these things. Morale soon significantly decreased

at the agency because of the separation between the alleged leaders

and their followers.

In contrast, another government leader took over an environment

with a negative culture. This leader took painstaking efforts to ensure

he became the in-group prototype. Prior to his arrival, executives

maintained separate eating quarters almost as a line of demarcation

between those who have power and those who don't. On the first day

he served, the leader went to the nonexecutive dining room and walked

to the back of the line. As you would expect, lower-ranking followers

motioned for the executive to go to the front of the line. The executive

declined and told his followers that he would wait in line just like

anyone else. The executive made additional changes to remove the traditional demarcation and wound up being the representative in-group prototype. The company performance and morale increased positively because of the actions taken by the leader.[50]

A boss who works on the belief that followers should do as I say but not as I do is doomed to never be a true leader. While followers are willing to accept certain benefits granted to a leader, they also expect the leader to represent their best interests. Being an in-group prototype requires a leader to recognize this fact. Are you walking the talk you prescribe for your followers?

---

[50] Abrashoff, D. (2002). *It's your ship: Management techniques from the best damn ship in the Navy*. New York, NY: Warner Books.

Are Your Grapes Really That Sour? How Cognitive Dissonance Impacts the Leader's Message

Are you stuck in the middle of your organizational hierarchy? Are there distinct problems that come from being in this position? Have you ever had to sell a policy or procedure to your followers even though you really didn't think the policy/procedure was best for the organization? Even though you didn't agree, did you do your best to get people to believe you supported the new initiative? If so, how effective do you think you were?

Leaders, especially those in the middle of organizations, are sometimes put in positions where they are supposed to support a view in which they don't necessarily agree. Psychologically, this situation is referred to as cognitive dissonance and it causes effects to the mind and body to include stress. Inasmuch as we naturally desire to be consistent in our beliefs, we look for ways to compensate for the dissonance.

Classically, cognitive dissonance is explained in a story called the

171

fox and the grapes. In the story, a fox is walking along when he sees a cluster of grapes hanging from a tree. The fox tries many different ways to reach the grapes to no avail. Finally, the fox walks away and says the grapes probably weren't good anyway. Making the statement about the ripeness of the grapes is the fox's way to reduce the dissonance between his desire for the grapes and the fact that he was unable to attain them. Can we apply this theory to leadership?

How many times have you attempted to persuade your executives to obtain or achieve something, and you were unsuccessful? Have you ever tried to convince your bosses that a policy or procedure won't work only to be overruled in the end? It is in these moments that our duty to be loyal to the organization causes us cognitive dissonance.

Chances are you did your best to sell the new policy/procedure, or you convinced your followers that whatever you wanted wasn't needed. Still, what is the probability that your followers sensed your true feelings? Professor Albert Mebrahian was able to ascertain the degree in which we receive information. When you are delivering your message, it is not the words you speak that convey your true feelings as they represent only 7 percent of the message heard. Rather, the bulk of the message you send is in the tone of your voice (38 percent) and nonverbal behaviors (55 percent). Therefore, even though you have fought through the mental part of cognitive dissonance by convincing yourself that the grapes probably weren't good anyway, your physical behaviors have betrayed you.

Dr. Joe Schafer, a professor at Southern Illinois University, conducted a study of police officers who attended the FBI National Academy and found that the top two traits they wanted in their leaders were honesty and integrity.[51] While there is certainly a need to be loyal and to accept not getting what you want, leaders need to be aware of how they communicate their message, both verbally and nonverbally, to maintain trust and integrity with their followers. The next time you get stuck in the midst of cognitive dissonance, it may not be the words that betray you, but rather the message you send with your body.

---

[51] Schafer, J. (2013). *Effective leadership in policing: Successful traits and habits.* Durham, NC: Carolina Academic Press.

Michael Bret Hood

ABOUT THE AUTHOR

In 2011, Michael "Bret" Hood was chosen to be part of a select team dedicated to developing new executive leadership development programs for the FBI. Drawing on his 25 years of experience as a special agent, supervisor and leader in the FBI, Bret took new and unique approaches to designing, developing, and implementing completely interactive instructional blocks designed to leverage the personal experiences of participants to drive learning. For his efforts, Bret received FBI Director awards for innovation and knowledge.

Bret has served as an adjunct professor of leadership for the University of Virginia teaching leadership and ethics course on both the undergraduate and graduate level. As an advanced master instructor and facilitator for the FBI, Bret created ten-week innovative and completely interactive programs to further the leadership development of domestic and international law enforcement executives who attended the prestigious FBI National Academy. To date, Bret has also led approximately 50 United States delegations to foreign countries to instruct and share knowledge with our foreign law enforcement counterparts. This book is designed to provide an experience similar to Bret's leadership classes with the goal being to provoke thought, question perceptions and perspectives, engage in deep self-assessment, and most of all.....to have fun. Bret continues to travel the world training public and private sector entities on leadership as well as financial crime and other topics through his web site, www.21puzzles.com. Bret also maintains a presence on LinkedIn at https://www.linkedin.com/in/michael-bret-hood-00b58b25.